VISITING KENYA

VISITING KENYA

John Brigden

B. T. Batsford Ltd, London

To Helen

Line drawings by Sally Harding

Maps by Robert F. Brien

*Photographs by Jeremy
and John Brigden*

First published 1987
© John Brigden 1987

ISBN 0 7134 5336 2

Printed in Great Britain by Butler & Tanner Ltd
Frome, Somerset
for the publishers,
B. T. Batsford Ltd,
4 Fitzhardinge Street,
London, W1H 0AH

Contents

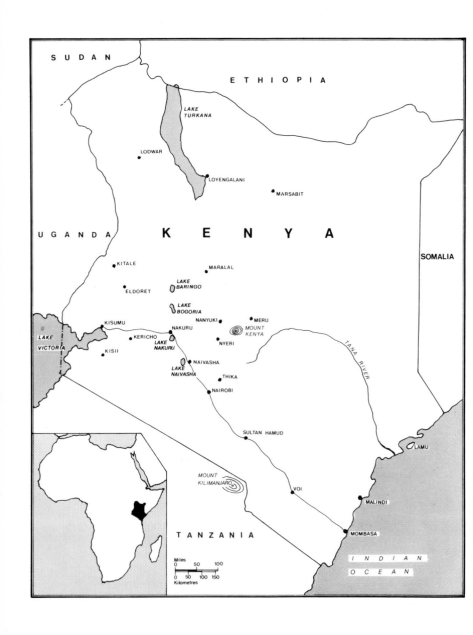

KENYA – General Map

1 The Pearl of Africa

Africa is a smooth, well-rounded stone, worn down over the ages by the footsteps of the oldest peoples in the world. Here is the place where man pulled himself up to break away from the animal kingdom. In the heart of this land is East Africa, geographically made up of Kenya and Tanzania but politically including Uganda. Kenya, though, is the open door through which the splendours of this unique part of the world can be seen and appreciated.

This is not an overcrowded country but a big, wide land with low horizons and large dramatic skies. Under this top-heavy canvas, usually blue sky and brown earth, man and animals live in an unusual harmony. In the country areas they live almost shoulder to shoulder, man and animal united in the struggle to survive in a hostile environment. In the towns life is quite different: here the animals don't often intrude (although the occasional lion has been seen scavenging in Nairobi during times of drought) but the open spaces give way to an overcrowded environment. Kenya has one of the world's fastest growing populations and most of these births are in the towns.

Although visitors will not usually come across the poorest parts of towns like Nairobi and Mombasa they will be conscious of the crush. Despite the signs there is no such thing as 'full'; there is always room for just one more on the bus or in the restaurant.

Most people arrive via Nairobi or Mombasa, two cities entirely different from each other except for the street names, of which there are a limited number. Nairobi looks the capital city it is with its modest skyscrapers piercing the broad skyline. It is a frontier town made good, but sometimes has a tendency to slip back to its former self. It is a colourful town which makes the most of its tourist clientele, the business centre of the country and it has one of the best climates on earth.

A lion roars a warning to visitors at Nairboi's National Park.

Mombasa is the main port for the country, has a much longer history and was even mentioned by Ptolemy in the second century A.D.; it was then called Tonikw. It would probably have been the capital city if only its climate had been a bit more temperate.

The coastline is all you would want of a tropical coast. Palm trees sway in a gentle, cooling breeze while a warm sea laps against the golden sands protected by a coral reef – another source of income for the local inhabitants, who organise dives and viewing trips for the eager tourists.

Take the 480 km (300 mile) trip to Nairobi from Mombasa and the difference in climate is dramatic, accounted for mostly by the altitude of Nairobi, which is 1500 m (5000 ft) above sea level.

hand in November Nairobi has 2.5 cm (around one inch) while Mombasa has 5–10 cm (between two and four inches). The wet seasons on the coast are really January and February and July and August. But, whatever the time of year, the rains are always welcome in this part of the world.

As for temperatures, in Nairobi it tends to hover around 18°–24°C (65°–75°F) all year round, although March can be a little hotter. Mombasa and the coastline are always hot. From November to the end of April it is around 30°C (80°–90°F), while the rest of the year it is around 24°–27°C (75°–80°F).

However, to counteract the heat there is invariably a cool wind blowing off the Indian Ocean, plenty of shady palm trees, and at all the hotels the service is geared towards iced drinks. You will inevitably try the local beer, aptly named Tusker, which is excellent cooled, and most of the international soft drinks are available. However, try the fresh fruit juice mixes, which are both refreshing and good for you.

A word of warning about the heat, which is intense. Even if you are used to holidays in the Greek islands, or around the Mediterranean, don't assume you can stay in the sun all day. It is as well to follow the advice of the country's tourist board, which recommends that at first you limit your sunbathing to around 20 minutes at a stretch, and that you stay longer only when you have become accustomed to the heat. You can buy suntan lotion there but it is cheaper at home; take plenty with you. You will need it even when you are just wandering around the game parks.

Despite the generally high temperatures it can become quite cool at night, particularly in the higher areas, so be prepared and take along a pullover and some warmer clothing. It won't get cold, unless you are unlucky, but it may get cool.

Farming

Kenya is not an industrial country and does not have any known significant mineral wealth. Land is therefore the most important natural resource the country has for the generation of economic wealth. But land is a scarce resource in Kenya: only 17 per cent is suitable for agriculture without any irrigation.

Agriculture, with tourism, is the mainstay to Kenya's economy and directly contributes over a third of the country's gross domestic product. It still accounts for the jobs of the larger part of the

A British Airways jumbo jet en route to Nairobi.

population and supplies most of Kenya's exports. The economy is one of the most advanced and diversified in Eastern and Central Africa. Essential foodstuffs are widely grown although the government encourages the planting of cash crops including coffee, rice, tea, cotton, sugar cane, maize, wheat and sisal. Coffee is the largest single crop, employing more than 200,000 of Kenya's labour force.

Kenya is also the largest producer of quality tea in the entire African continent and its production is now dominated by small-scale farmers, a result of the Government's efforts towards redistribution of land.

Products such as pineapples, flowers and vegetables have become a major export industry and bring in much valuable foreign currency.

Kenya also has a large and expanding livestock industry. Most parts of the country are suitable for ranching and there is an important dairy industry in the higher rainfall areas. Large quantities of excellent beef are exported to neighbouring countries, the Middle East and Europe. Kenya also produces some of the finest and most tender lamb, as well as delicious quality bacon in the Uplands Bacon Factory, almost a must for breakfast at any hotel.

The Kenya Cooperative Creameries process and distribute milk in most parts of the country.

In addition to these principal crops and livestock products, Kenya produces large amounts of beans, potatoes, cashew nuts, macadamia nuts, onions and fruit, and the country's markets are extremely full with a wide variety of vegtables.

2 A History of Kenya

Most Europeans know very little about the history of Kenya. Most British people probably think it was one of those countries that was taken over in the course of building the largest empire on earth, a positive step into Africa which assured a foothold in this part of the world. The story is, of course, much more complicated. Its history is tied up with such names as Livingstone and Thompson, with India and a railway, as well as Lord Delamere and Jomo Kenyatta. It is connected with the slave trade, its abolition, Arabs, Zanzibar, Oman and Uganda.

The Portuguese Arrive

In fact it was the Portuguese who were the first Europeans to taken an interest in this part of Africa. It was occupied as a strategic point for their trade routes to India which, from around 1500, was partly Portuguese. It was discovered by Vasco da Gama in 1497 on his famous voyage to the East. He found a thriving civilisation, whose people were called the Zinj, occupying the region. Portugal demanded the supply of fresh water and supplies for its ships, as well as the fealty of the the citizens. As far as the population was concerned the supply of stores and water was the cheap part, it was the fealty that came dear: Portugal demanded annual tribute payments in gold.

There was never peace for long between subjects and subjugators, so in 1593 work began on Fort Jesus, the largest fortification on the coast, but unhappily for the Portuguese it was not the security they had hoped it might be. In 1631 one Yusuf bin Hassan – also known as Don Geronimo – gathered 3,000 Arab and Swahili soldiers together and massacred every Portuguese in Mombasa, taking possession of the fort. Four years later it was back in the hands of Portugal, but the

Guns which the Portuguese once used to defend Fort Jesus, at Mombasa, are now a silent reminder of a violent past.

end of the Portuguese rule was in sight. They had lost Ormuz, a town in the Persian Gulf, in 1622 to the Persian army, and then in 1651 their stronghold of Muscat fell to the forces of Omani Arabs who had previously made it their capital. This gave new hope to the peoples of East Africa and for the next 70 years, during which time Mombasa was exchanges like a baton in a relay race, there was little peace. The Portuguese finally left in 1729, never to return.

The only lasting evidence of their occupation is, according to legend, that they buried the pod of a Baobab tree with their dead, so lying under many of these in the area could be the bones of a Portuguese soldier or sailor.

The Omanis Take Over

The Omanis who had supplied much of the firepower and money to the Kenyan rulers, filled the vacuum left by the Europeans and, regarding the coast as theirs by conquest, continued to collect taxes for the next century, although it took most of their energies not to have a repeat of the Portuguese experience.

In 1799 Napoleon landed in Egypt and courted the Imam of Muscat, Seyyid Sultan bin Ahmed, whose little state of Muscat (Oman) was a vital point in the link with India, which Britain was in the process of acquiring. However, just a few months earlier Seyyid had signed a treaty with Britain preventing the French from landing or docking at the port. On such small events is history made, because not only did it secure India for the British but also led to their involvement with East Africa and another empire. A year later the Imam consented to the posting of 'an English gentleman of respectability' as a full-time British agent in Muscat, thus enrolling it as a client state of Britain.

The responsibility for Muscat brought with it the East African territories but it was nearly a century and 29 governments later before the British finally took the plunge, unwillingly still, to rule East Africa.

The Slave Trade

Trading created the climate for exploration into the heart of this part of Africa. Ivory and slaves were the attractions and often it needed just one two-year trip to the interior to earn enough money to retire for the rest of your life. These caravans, in the name of Seyyid Said, or the Sultan of Zanzibar as he was now known, opened up the interior and, on paper at least, made him owner of an empire covering a quarter of Africa, although in practice he was not interested in its government. The slave trade, though, was devastating the African continent. According to whose account you read, between 250,000 and one million slaves a year were being sent to the coast. It is estimated that four out of five died on the journey to Zanzibar before they were transported to Oman and elsewhere. At the time that Seyyid Said moved to Zanzibar the British conscience about slaving was beginning to stir; it had already been illegal in Britain since 1772 and efforts to free the rest of the world from slavery began shortly afterwards in earnest.

In 1812 and 1815 letters were sent to Seyyid Said from Bombay suggesting he might want to help Britain in reducing the slave trade, but the requests were ignored. It was another seven years before another approach was made, which culminated in the Moresby Treaty, cutting off the supply of slaves to India and Mauritius.

Later, further measures gave British warships the right to intercept slave dhows, mostly operated by north African Arabs, but the trade continued. Between 1867 and 1869 40,000 slaves were traded; the British navy only managed to intercept and free 2,645 of them.

In the 1870s and 1880s people began to feel that edict alone was not enough to abolish the devilish trade, but that the source of the trade—the hinterland behind Mombasa—must be occupied by the British to stem the raw materials of slavery, and so British involvement in Kenya was deepened.

The Scramble for Africa

In 1884 a young German named Carl Peters had arrived in Dar es Salaam, collected a caravan together and headed out into the unknown and succeeded in getting several tribal chiefs to sign a piece of paper ceding their territory to Germany. This action the British could not let go unanswered as it encompassed most of the territory in East Africa; this was nominally controlled by the Sultan of Zanzibar who had been promised protection by the British.

In December of the following year a conference was convened in Europe in which spheres of influence in Africa were delineated. This part of East Africa was neatly sliced up, giving the Germans the southern half, roughly the country of present-day Tanzania, with the British getting the northern part, Kenya; Uganda was nominally in the British sphere but not officially designated. But the catch in all this was that to have your sphere recognised you had to show effective occupation – something the British had been remarkably reluctant to do, particularly as this was going to cost the British taxpayer money. The way round this was to interest the private sector into taking the risk through a chartered company, with the Government helping out with loans. In 1887 the British East Africa Association was formed, a year later obtaining a royal charter and changing its name to the Imperial British East Africa Company (I.B.E.A.).

It immediately started work, building bridges, trading points and a road which eased the path of porters and which eventually reached the Great Rift Valley.

Germany briefly gained control of Uganda, but handed it over to Britain by treaty. In 1894, following a survey by the British government, Uganda was finally made a British Protectorate, and to administer it a railway had to be built to the coast – through Kenya.

On 11 December 1895 George Whitehouse, chief engineer for the railway line, landed in sultry tropical Mombasa to begin his 921 kilometre, 572 mile long line. It miraculously reached Lake Victoria in December 1901 and was completed on 17 September 1904 at a cost of £5.5 million. It was instrumental in eventually putting a stop to the slave trade, and opened up Uganda and the land in-between.

The Protectorate of British East Africa finally gave way to the Kenya Colony Protectorate in 1920, but it wasn't until 1944 that the first African was nominated as a member of the Legislative Council. Soon after, the Kenya African Union was formed and the late Mzee Jomo Kenyatta was made President in 1947. His sole aim was to gain independence from Britain and to this end was part of the Mau Mau rising which terrorised the country, particularly between 1952 and 1959. The first African elections were held in 1957, after which changes in the composition of the Kenyan Government came steadily. By 1960 the Legislative Council had an African majority and it was in the same year that the Kenya African National Union (K.A.N.U.) was formed. Later, when Kenyatta was released from detention, he was unanimously accepted as the leader of the party.

Three years later K.A.N.U., among several other parties, contested the 1963 General Elections and won, later leading the country to full independence. In August 1978 Kenyatta, the father of Kenya, died and he was succeeded by the present President, Daniel arap T. Moi, who has developed the theme of unity among the tribes, to rule over one of the most stable and progressive countries in Africa.

3 Culture

East Africa has been called the cradle of mankind, a name given to it following the discoveries of early man by Dr Louis and Mary Leakey on the Kenya/Tanzania border. Their son Richard was also bitten by the archaeological bug and it was a dig led by him which discovered the remains of man's oldest cousin. It is a skull about 2.8 million years old from the shores of Lake Turkana in the north of Kenya. There is a small museum at the site in the Sibiloi National Park, which also houses examples of other fossils. Richard Leakey first saw the site from the air in 1967 while conducting a survey, but it was not until 1972 that he finally pieced together 300 fragments of a skull, now named 1470 Man after its catalogue number.

Recent discoveries have been able to shed more light on man's ancestors. In 1984 the most important find since 1470 Man was made when Kamoya Kimeua, a Kenyan fossil hunter, turned up a small piece of human-like skull near Lake Turkana. Further digging revealed an almost complete skeleton, dated at around 1.6 million years old. It is of a boy and of a species which could be a forefather of *homo erectus* – our own ancestors. The importance of the find wasn't just its age but the fact it was a whole skeleton; previously finds had been only of the odd skull or piece of bone.

The area also has a number of other surprises. For example, at the Research Project near Koobi Fora there are the quasi-human remains of Lucy, a lady 3 million years old. Other discoveries include the remains of 30 hitherto unknown species of antelope as well as turtles larger than any seen today. In 1979 seven footprints were found and dated radiometrically as 1.5 million years old and identified as those of *homo erectus*.

Little is known about the intervening years, but it is widely accepted that the peoples who now inhabit the land mostly arrived between the fourteenth and nineteenth centuries.

The African population of the country amounts to nearly 98 per cent, with the remaining 2 per cent comprised mostly of Asians, but including Europeans and Arabs – the earliest non-African settlers and the original slave traders.

There were once probably around 80,000 Europeans, mostly British, in Kenya, following the lead given by Lord Delamere, the founding father of Kenyan agriculture, whose estate is still largely intact. The numbers quickly diminished after independence in 1963, although there is still a sizeable expatriate population. In fact Europeans still run many of the estates and farms, hotels and businesses and at the same time are giving valuable training to the Kenyans.

Many Asians were brought in by the British from India to build the Uganda Railway. Some died from malaria and other diseases while others later returned to the sub-continent, but enough stayed to form a hard-working and prosperous minority, which is now generally envied by the Africans. There are fears in many people's minds that a repeat of Uganda's mass deportation could happen in Kenya too, but at present this looks unlikely as Kenya claims to be a multi-racial society, and the administration is keen to preserve political and economic stability.

Both Europeans and Asians tend to keep themselves apart from Kenyan society and it is only the Arabs who have been truly assimilated, in the process creating the Swahili language – which, along with English, is the national tongue.

The Africans comprise about forty different tribes, although they can broadly be placed into four groups: Bantu, Nilotic, Hamitic and Nilo-Hamitic.

The Bantu make up some of the largest tribes in Kenya and have traditionally been agriculturalists, usually cultivating the lower slopes of the mountains and highlands.

The Nilotic group is almost entirely composed of the Luo tribe, and lives around the north, mainly on the shores of Lake Turkana.

The Hamitics are the nomads of the north, unconcerned with agriculture and keeping only sheep, goats and camels, which represent their wealth and standing.

The Nilo-Hamitic group (not related to the Nilotic or Hamitic groups) represents the greatest attraction for the tourist as they include all the famous tribes, including the Masai and Samburu, who are both colourful and rich in ceremony.

There are two tribes who do not fit into these neat groups, the

Dorobo from the Mau Forest and the El Molo, who roam the barren shores of Lake Turkana. They were probably in the area we now know as Kenya long before the others but were subdued by the invasion from the north of these other four groups.

The Masai

The Masai are distinguished by their character, their good manners, and their impressive physical presence. Their fundamental belief is that all the cattle on earth belong to them. It is a religious belief based on the idea that Enkai, the sky god, was once one with earth. When the earth and the sky separated Enkai sent down to the Masai all the cattle, by means of the wild fig tree, now a holy tree for the Masai. This belief is interpreted quite literally by the Masai, although these days they graciously lend them out to other peoples and tribes.

'I hope your cattle are well' is a greeting often heard among the Masai, and quite rightly so, as practical as well as mystical beliefs bind the Masai to their cattle. The milk, the blood and the meat of the cattle also feed the tribes. Hides provide the mattresses of their bedding, the sandals for their feet and mats for them to sit on.

The live animals are essential for the marriage bonds, establishing homes and families. Cattle pay fines to re-establish social harmony and are the sacrifices for the most important ceremonial occasions.

Keeping the cattle and other livestock in fresh water and pasture as well as safe from predators, both human and non-human, is a full time job for members of the tribe. Leisure time has therefore been developed into an art.

Life for the Masai is one long celebration. From birth and up to, but not including, death, every event, other than the mundane ones, and each significant change in the individual's life, is a cause for celebration.

The other aspects of their life which characterise the Masai culture is their age grouping system, the red ochre worn on their bodies and the long hair worn by the junior warriors, the coils of wire on the limbs of the women and the loaf-shaped houses forming the scattered villages across the grasslands.

The Masai adaption of the age-group system consists of junior warrior, senior warrior, junior elder and senior elder. Each genera-

Masai children dressed up for the visitors to Mayas Ranch, north of Nairobi.

tion of men constitutes an age set which passes through each grade in succession.

After circumcision boys become men and warriors – this grouping is the famous *moran*, who are better known these days for their levitation dance where they seem miraculously to jump many feet into the air with minimal effort. Previously the age sets lasted 12 to 15 years but now they have been reduced.

The duties of the junior warriors used to be to provide a fighting force as well as to serve the community in times of domestic crisis. When the age set has completed its service as junior warriors it graduates to senior, normally marries and becomes a sort of home guard – or used to be – for a period of about fifteen years. The junior elders finally assume full possession of their cattle, previously held in trust. Both elder age grades make up the traditional administrative body of the Masai.

Traditionally the Masai have neither headman, chiefs, nor any system of centralised authority; instead, public opinion sways the arguments – a sort of democracy.

The Masai have a reputation of being the original noble savages, although in fact they are a pastoral people. Apart from herding, a small percentage of the people have turned to cultivation, either as a token pursuit to supplement what is basically a milk and (occasionally) meat diet, or as a commercial proposition to supply barley to breweries.

The Masai get their name from their speech – Maa – and inhabit both Kenya and Tanzania, with most of their territory being in the latter country and most of their population in the former.

It is likely that the Masai came into Kenya somewhere to the west of Lake Turkana. They then spread into and across the country; the expansion slowed in the seventeenth century, and by the eighteenth century they had migrated as far south as what is now Tanzania.

From the time the Masai reached the Rift Valley, about five hundred years ago, they expanded across Kenya and Tanzania with a force out of all proportion to their numbers, becoming the dominant peoples in East Africa. They were formidable foes indeed and myth did little to exaggerate their powers. In the absence of documented numbers it has been estimated that at the peak of their powers in the last century their total population did not exceed 50,000. Around 10,000 of them would have been men available for active fighting duty – a powerful force in an empty land.

In the last decade of the ninteenth century they nearly succumbed to diseases of the outside world – cholera and smallpox – and also suffered heavily when a serious outbreak of rinderpest decimated their herds.

Early in this century they confronted yet another foe, the European settler, who evicted them, mostly by treaty, from their lands, although they are now one of the richest tribes in Africa.

Today they face the problem of limited lands for a growing human and stock population.

The Samburu

The Samburu have similar attitudes to their cattle and lifestyle as their more southerly cousins, the Masai. They settled their present lands around the Maralal (lands further to the west than those they were evicted from by the Turkana people) during the times of the Masai expansion across Kenya around five hundred years ago.

Some of the finest scenery in Kenya lies within their district, including the mountains of the Mathews Range, the Ndoto Mountains and Mount Nyira as well as the Lbarta Plains, the Horr Valley and the Upper Suiyia River. The tribe enjoy the beauties of the countryside as much as anyone and almost every settlement has been constructed with this in mind, their locations affording the best perspective of whatever panorama presents itself.

Although they now accept the name Samburu, it is not the name by which they traditionally knew themselves, which was Loikop. Samburu, appropriately, means butterfly. The young warriors appear strikingly effeminate, with refined features and almost fragile slenderness, although this appearance is deceptive. However, it is compounded by their bodily adornment; the young warriors create decorative designs around their eyes and wear their hair immaculately plainted, long or in a bun. Unlike their fellow *moran* among the Masai, the young Samburu men do not smear their entire body with ochre, but make triangular designs down their chests and backs.

But, like their Masai cousins, they have a pastoral economy, reflected in the diet, which has milk as a staple. Meat, as in all pastoral societies, is rarely eaten, although every animal is eventually consumed. Ceremonial celebrations, of which there are many, are the occasions for slaughtering the animals; ocasionally one is killed during a dry spell, purely for survival.

The Samburu *moran* have not acquired a reputation for being fearsome fighters, like those of the Masai, but they have always been

Samburu moran in formation.

important in deterring raiders and for the preservation of the stock. In addition to the *moran* age group there are two others – boys and elders.

The age system is one part of the Samburu social structure, the other being the clan system, although the clans tend to be scattered rather than concentrated territorially. The Samburu tribe are also held together by the brotherhoods – brotherhoods by descent, by bond, and by joking bond (informal). There is also *olpiroi*, the firestick relationship, in which a senior age set, the firestick elders, are responsible for the moral education and the creation of a sense of respect – to facilitate control – among an existing age set of *moran*.

However, the real governing force is consensus, and not the dictates of a select élite. Chiefs, headmen and other colonial government appointees only emerged in the 1920s and have not affected the tribe's underlying traditions.

Njemps

The Njemps are Masai-speaking relatives of the Samburu who settled near Lake Baringo, adopting the name of the area and becoming agriculturalists. They occupy the area to the south and east of the lake, a land from which Samburu oral tradition claims the Samburu migrated in around 1840.

Just before the Second World War the Njemps population was estimated at just 1600, despite their success in the previous century in selling their produce to the caravans which stopped at Lake Baringo to resupply before heading off to Uganda, Zaire and the interior.

The land around Lake Baringo is not very fertile so the Njemps created an irrigation system. It was first noted in 1910 but for some reason was abandoned by the tribe in 1920 and not revived until 1940. Today they continue their agriculture but use both traditional and modern methods to overcome the limitations of the soil.

Although they primarily work on the land, fishing is another important aspect of their economy. For this they have constructed a special kind of canoe made from the local ambatch wood. It grows around Baringo and is similar to balsa wood. Separate sections of ambatch are bound together to form a peaked bow and an open stern. A separate deck is also constructed and inserted into the shell. It looks a little flimsy but is extremely buoyant and capable of transporting small stock across the lake.

In spite of their agricultural prosperity the Njemps are also adept at attracting tourists, particularly from the local camps around the lake. They also possess a few cattle, from stock acquired during the period of British rule. They do have some similarities with their Samburu and Masai brothers in that they have a *moran* system, they dress and decorate themselves in Masai fashion, and their songs and high jumping are similar.

After they settled by Lake Baringo the Njemps have progressively, and perhaps inevitably, become a mixed group, intermarrying with the neighbouring Tugen. Culturally, though, and physically, the Masai remain dominant among the Njemps, and today they constitute the largest group of Masai speaking cultivators in Kenya.

Luo

The Luo come from the Lake Victoria area of Kenya and are one group whose migration is relatively easily traced from the southern confluence of the Nile. Their dispersal began in the fifteenth century, and they arrived in Kenya between 1500 and the mid-1600s.

They are an extremely charming race with a broad smile and a welcoming nature, although in their time they have been known as ferocious warriors. Aspects of Luo culture have changed considerably in the last quarter of this century. They continue to farm, herd and fish, but they have entered politics, the professions and commercial life in large numbers. That they have adapted to changes so effectively is due in part to the fact that the Luo were in a great state of flux for generations preceding the arrival of the Western influences, excellent preparation for the even vaster changes that were to come.

However, some of the traditions remain, including the segregation, at puberty, of the boys and the girls into their formal sleeping arrangements. Marriage is of two types still: *por*, which is elopement and considered shameful, and *meko*, the traditional marriage involving numerous ceremonies. Bridal wealth is still given in the form of cattle, although these days it is more likely to be one or two head rather than 15 to 20.

Traditionally the husband built his wife her own house after she gave birth to their first child. The house of the senior wife was located across from the main entrance to the husband's residence. Other wives lived on either side of the first wife.

Despite the Luo being agriculturalists they are still extremely attached to their cattle, and when they talk of a rich man it means someone with cattle. A poor man is one who has little or no livestock, no matter how full his granaries are. The thinking behind it is that crops may fail, but cattle and livestock will still live; children are a measure of prosperity, they should fare better on milk than on grain.

The cattle also played another important role in the lives of the Luo, as it was on the oxen that the young warriors rode into battle – one of the few tribes to use this alternative source of motive force.

Besides that the cattle provide milk, butter, meat, sleeping mats, sandals, drumskins, shield covers, bow strings, dung fuel and dung wall plaster. More than you would ever get from an ear of corn!

Kamba

We know, from archaeological evidence, that the Bantu-speaking peoples have been in East Africa for the past 2000 years.

In the western parts of East Africa, and around Lake Victoria, iron working and the use of iron tools were probably introduced by these early Bantus, who cleared large tracts of land for agriculture.

Among the most famous of the Bantu tribes are the Kamba, who occupy the area to the south of the Tana River called Ukamba. With the exception of a small group, all the Kamba agree in their oral traditions that the plains around Mount Kilimanjaro were the earliest known region of origin for the tribe. Europeans who recorded this tradition in writing heard it as far back as 1849, when the tribe's collective memory was fresher. Initial settlements in the Kilimanjaro region may have been established by the late 1400s and there may still have existed some settlements in the region in the early 1600s.

Originally the Kamba were probably semi-nomadic. They were also pastoralists and most Kamba oral tradition claims they were once cattle herders, rich in stock. However, by the time the first Europeans arrived this was no more than legend and there was considerable evidence that during their nomadic existence they had survived on hunting and collecting edible plants and roots. At this time grain or vegetable cultivation was not practised.

Their exodus from Kilimanjaro began towards the end of the sixteenth century with the arrival of the more warlike Masai. First they moved north to the Chyulu Hills, but they were too rocky and lacked adequate surface water, so they then headed off to the Mbooni Hills in the centre of the Ukamba highlands. At Mbooni (the place of the buffalo) they finally started to settle into a semi-sedentary life of a more agricultural than pastoral nature. This forested region had fertile soil, high rainfall and protection from other tribes. The forested hill habitat was explored and exploited: iron was extracted from riverbeds, reeds were used as arrow shafts, bark for poison tips and plants used for food and medicine.

It was during this period in Mbooni that the institutional life of the Kamba was established – particularly the clan structure. The Kamba continued to expand their territory until about 1780, and from this time until around 1850 the Kamba emerged as the outstanding trading people in East Africa, their most valuable commodity being ivory, which they exchanged at the coast for trade goods. This economic pursuit created a proficient class of hunters with highly developed techniques for killing elephants.

By the mid-nineteenth century life was altering and a feature of Kamba culture was its state of flux. Change, predicted by fortune tellers, soon came with the arrival of Europeans and the East Africa Company station at Machakos, the building of the railway and colonial rule. The changing Kamba culture was easily able to cope and it wasn't long before the tribe assumed a dominant role in contemporary Kenya.

These days the Kamba influence can also be seen in the numerous artifacts that are available throughout Kenya. For instance, many of the wood carvings seen in almost every tourist shop and stall originate from the Kamba area, although these are the least traditional of their crafts. Others which are more traditional include wooden spoons, ladles and three-legged stools. However, the most spectacular manifestation of Kamba culture is their dance, characterised by leaping, the flinging of dancers into the air and acrobatics. Unfortunately, with the exception of official functions and in tourist areas – where it is only done moderately well – this dancing is rarely seen these days.

Kikuyu

The most successful recent cultural adaptation of all the peoples of Kenya has been displayed by the Kikuyu, who are now numerically the largest group in the country. they were also the group mainly responsible for the attainment of Kenya's independence. Even now their influence in government, commerce, and most other fields of contemporary life surpass that of any other group. Traditionally they occupied the central highlands, which extend from Mount Kenya in

Tribal elder, no longer brightly dressed, in deference to his position in society.

the north towards Nairobi and from the Kikuyu Escarpment and the Aberdare Mountains in the West towards Ukamba in the East.

The Kikuyu people are an amalgam of different groups, typifying the histories of so many peoples and cultures in Kenya. Intermarriage between the Kikuyu and Masai was quite frequent. (Mzee Jomo Kenyatta, the first president of Kenya and a Kikuyu, had both Masai blood and ties: his paternal grandmother was a Masai and an aunt married a notable Masai).

They were an expanding people, in terms of territory and population, when the British arrived and they were prepared to use this mobility to adapt to and exploit the changes to come. To understand the extensive involvement of the Kikuyu people in the economic sector today, it is helpful to look at their history and the importance of the emergence of the work ethic. Having settled in an environment ideal for agriculture, the Kikuyu exploited it to the full, producing food far in excess of what they needed for themselves. In the nineteenth century they put this to good use by supplying Swahili caravans and European expeditions with essential food. They also carried on regional trade with their neighbours, including the Kamba and the Masai, whom the Kamba had made junior partners in their activities. When the Kamba declined as traders, the Kikuyu took over.

In the traditional culture of the Kikuyu people one is able to detect two features which are characteristic of contemporary Kenya: a fair democratic political system, and a productive, expanding free-market economy. However, these features are by no means exclusively Kikuyu; they are shared by most of the people in Kenya. At present, as the numerically largest group of Kenya, the Kikuyu people are the custodians of both these traits.

Embu

The highland Embu are closely related to their neighbours, the Kikuyu. They share common origins, although in both tribes these are mixed. According to legend the Embu are the descendants of a man named Mwene-Ndega. He took a wife, and their first two children were a boy named Kembu and a girl named Werimba. The children committed incest and were expelled from their home, so they found a new home nearby where they lived as man and wife. Their children established homes throughout Embu country, and became known as the children of Kembu, or Embu for short.

During the early Embu days tradition says that it was primarily a hunting-gathering economy, one which the forest environment encouraged. Then they started to grow millet, sorghum and root crops. In the last half of the ninenteenth century coastal traders introduced maize. Livestock entered the economy mostly through trade.

At first the Embu lived in caves or hollow trees. Shelter changed with the economy; forest dwellings were abandoned for round houses with thatched roofs. These days most Embu houses are more European in style, being rectangular and covered with corrugated iron.

Traditionally the basic unit for the Embu was the family with the father as head of the household. Next up in importance came the settlement council, the clan and the council of warrior leaders. Higher up still were the councils of justice, dispensing all forms of justice, settling disputes and calling on lesser councils to enact its decisions. The thread running through all was the age sets which made and proclaimed laws governing behaviour and social practice.

Most of the population is concentrated in the Embu district – south east of Mount Kenya in Eastern Province. As agriculturalists the good soil is important to them, with the best land being found between 4000 and 7000 feet above sea level, being mostly volcanic.

Pokomo

The best known of the coastal and hinterland tribes are the Pokomo who occupy the banks of the Lower Tana from the coast upstream to Garissa. A common Pokomo village varies in size from 10 to 50 houses in a compact grouping. From a distance it resembles a cluster of haystacks.

The Pokomo are an agricultural people, although they do some fishing as well. To make the most of their land they have developed a method of crop distribution. On the banks of the river they plant coarse bananas and sugar cane; on the lowlands behind there is rice; and on the higher ground they grow maize and beans. This intensive agriculture's aim is to produce a surplus, not just because of the unpredictable nature of the environment but also because social obligations are paid in agricultural products. This custom has guaranteed the even distribution of surplus production so that no-one goes wanting – a form of welfare state.

Apart from their use as food the agricultural products give the people a place in life. In order to maintain status one has to be able to

Crafts, here displayed by the road side, are a major source of income for the tribes.

feed guests well, for entertainment as well as at such occasions as funerals. Even bridewealth is given in the form of food. Also, in the past, one was able to buy one's way up the social scale, often by giving a feast for one's immediate elders. It was, and still is, a very structured society.

The women are responsible for the agricultural production, under the direction of their menfolk, who devote their time to fishing and, in the past, to the hunting of crocodiles, hippoes and elephants.

Hippoes were hunted for their meat and fat, while the elephants were mainly hunted for their ivory, which was probably sent down river to Lamu. Today there is still trade with Lamu but it now takes the form of woven mats and other crafts.

Mijikenda

The Mijikenda land begins just south of the Tana River and continues down the coastal hinterland in a 30–40 km (19–25 mile) wide strip. The coast itself, a very narrow plain, has been occupied by the Arabs and the Swahili for a long time, but behind that rises a 150–250 m (500–800 ft) high ridge which turns into a rolling plateau, which is the area the Mijikenda inhabit.

The name Mijikenda means nine villages, and the tribe does actually consist of nine groups. Before the beginning of this century, though, they had no group name, nor did they have corporate institutions. However, after settling down in their present lands as individual groups they eventually joined forces in an agricultural life with a limited amount of livestock.

One curious feature is the apparently large size of the backsides of the women, reminiscent of the steatopygic Hottentot women. However, with the Mijikenda this is purely artificial as it is created by about forty metres of cloth folded and placed under their skirts.

4 General Information

Travel

Kenya has two main ports of entry by air – Jomo Kenyatta International Airport at Nairobi and Moi International Airport at Mombasa. Mombasa is also the main port of entry by sea.

At least twenty airlines fly to Kenya, either as a destination or a stop-over, usually for South Africa or Mauritius. From London the main carriers, and the only two direct ones, are British Airways and Kenya Airways. It is possible to obtain seats on other European airlines such as Swissair or KLM, but both involve two-stage flights via their respective home countries.

Kenya Airways is also the main domestic carrier in Kenya, flying between Malindi, Mombasa and Nairobi, but there are numerous small airstrips throughout the country and almost as many small operators, who invariably have room for you whether you have booked or not. At Nairobi there is also Wilson Airport, the third largest strip in Kenya, where most of the smaller flights go from, transporting visitors and businessmen the quick way to the game parks; if you have the time it is well worth a flight to Amboseli or the Masai Mara, where you may fly over the hippo pools which can have upwards of fifty hippos wallowing about. It's a fine sight from the air.

Visas

British passport holders do not require a visa, except those of Asian origin, who must also hold the equivalent of 4000 shillings in a convertible currency.

Holders of South African passports are refused admission unless they are passing through, as long as they don't leave the airport.

Visas are obtainable through Kenyan consular offices; in countries where there are no diplomatic relations, visas are issued through the British Embassy or Consulate.

Customs Regulations

As long as you are 16 years old or more then you are allowed to import 200 cigarettes or 50 cigars or 250 g of tobacco, one litre bottle of alcohol and half a litre of perfume. There are the usual restrictions on the import of fruit, seeds, plants, imitation pistols, etc., and naturally firearms and ammunition require a police permit. The export of gold and diamonds is prohibited and the export of ivory, coral and shells is severely restricted; you must show a certificate of purchase on exit.

On leaving the country you must pay an airport tax of $10 or the equivalent in foreign currency (i.e. not Kenyan shillings) – remember to keep some money for this as the customs officials are not amused by claims of ignorance of the levy.

Travel in Kenya

Apart from flying with the national carrier or independent companies, as mentioned, there a number of other ways of getting about.

Rail

At the last count there were 2647 km (1645 miles) of track in Kenya linking Uganda with the Mombasa coast, and serving such places as Kericho, Nanyuki and Kisumu. There is a sleeper service between Nairobi and Mombasa and Kisumu. Two trains travel nightly in each direction between Mombasa and Nairobi and the journey takes about thirteen hours. At one time this was the Rolls-Royce of train journeys in Africa, with silver service and food to match. Unfortunately both the service and the carriages have fallen on hard times, although at the time of writing (1986) some new carriages were being introduced which will at least make it a comfortable journey once again. The silver service, personal tables and chairs, and table lights are, alas, lost for ever; the new dining car is standard issue.

However, don't be put off. It is an experience of a lifetime leaving Nairobi at dusk at about seven o'clock, gently pulling through the outskirts and into the bush. If you wake early enough you may be lucky in seeing elephant or giraffe as the train passes through the Tsavo National Park. As the train approaches Mombasa the heat

Take the overnight train from Nairobi to Mombasa for a really memorable journey.

builds up, as do the crowds of youngsters lining the track to wave at you.

When you leave your carriage in Mombasa after breakfast the heat is, naturally, tremendous. Perspiration is immediate although to look at some of the locals you might think it is the middle of winter. They are often, at this early hour, wrapped up in brightly-coloured scarves and pullovers and seem oblivious to the heat.

Roads
Of the 160,000 kilometres (100,000 miles) of roads throughout the country only a little more than 5000 are tarmac, with the rest being

Sometimes the road seems to go on forever. This one runs dead straight for 24 km (15 miles) and forms a boundary of the Tsavo West National Park.

marram (dirt) tracks. Many of the tracks are excellent, and because they are cheap to regrade are often better than the tarmac roads, although when wet can be very difficult for the inexperienced driver. Look out for what are called 'black cotton' roads as these are particularly treacherous in the wet. The tarmac roads connect Kenya to its neighbours and are usually the main trade routes.

If you do wish to drive you should get your own licence endorsed at the Road Transport Office, Gill House, Moi Avenue, Nairobi. If you don't want to go through what can be a lengthy procedure, obtain an International Driving Licence from the AA or RAC before you leave Britain. They do not require endorsement.

Driving is, of course, on the left as in Britain. You have to keep a wary eye out when driving in Kenya, as there is very little road discipline. Watch out for broken down cars, which are often parked awkwardly and usually have a few twigs or part of a bush lying on the road beside them. The rule for driving at night is *don't*. The danger is not animals, although it is not unknown for a car to hit the odd buffalo or elephant in the dark, it's that broken down cars are impossible to see until you are upon them, and that to break down in the middle of nowhere can be extremely dangerous. Also beware of pedestrians, approaching cars with a single headlight, cattle, and natural hazards such as a stream flowing across the road, a sand drift or enormous potholes. Lorries are a major hazard, day or night, as they are often overloaded and take a couple of miles to overtake each other. Discretion is the better part of valour here, and you should leave the road rather than expect one of the lorries to give way.

When driving into the more outlying areas you should take food and water with you as, in the event of a breakdown, it may be many hours before another vehicle passes along the road.

Always carry a map. There are excellent road maps of various scales available. Kenya is the only African country with a set of ordnance survey maps available – although they are not right up to date.

The Kenyan authorities have recently developed a liking for sleeping policemen, as well as toll booths, and these two often go together. You will also find numerous police road checks, so slow down; you will not be asked to stop as they are after overloaded lorries or Matatus (small private estate-type cars or combitaxis).

The Matatus are not recommended travelling for the visitor as they are always overcrowded and it is a relatively dangerous form of transport. It is not unusual for two to collide, prompting headlines

Crossing the equator can become an everyday occurence.

such as '32 killed in Matatu accident' – these are six-seater vehicles! 'Matatu' roughly translated means 'always room for three more'.

Buses are another unreliable form of transport, although they are better than the Matatus. They regularly ply the routes between Nairobi and Mombasa and are usually very crowded.

If you have to take an ordinary taxi in one of the towns consult the hotel management or a tour guide about the correct price, and always agree on the price before you start the journey.

Climate

Kenya sits astride the equator so has no seasons – just summer all year round with the occasional rainy season. The sun rises between 5.45 and 6.30 a.m. and sets roughly twelve hours later. It also rises and sets extremely quickly compared with more temperate latitudes. Don't expect a lingering sunset; it might be dramatic but it won't last long.

Overall Kenya has a superb climate and in the most popular up-country resorts it is neither too hot or too cold, with long, sun-filled days.

A sign at the Lake Baringo Club. I am assured that contrary to popular belief hippos don't panic if you come between them and water.

At the coast the temperature rarely falls below 22°C (72°F), and then only during the odd day in May, June or July, and even then it can never be described as cold. In August, September and October the temperature at Mombasa will be around 25°C (77°F), and during the rest of the year it will average 29° to 30°C (around 85°F). The humidity is high, around 75 per cent, which can make things very sticky, although fortunately there is generally a strong breeze blowing along the coast to keep you cool. The sun is always powerful, being almost vertically overhead, so be careful to break the sunbathing in gently as it is all too easy to end up with sunstroke or a badly burned skin, even if you consider yourself a hardened sunworshipper. Occasionally at night you may need a light pullover, particularly if the wind is blowing off the Indian Ocean.

As you go inland the altitude also rises, but don't be fooled by the cooler feel to the climate – the sun is still fierce, so take sensible precautions to suit your skin-type.

Because of the heat the body loses more fluid than in the European climate; make sure you drink plenty throughout the day.

As far as the rains are concerned, the long rains occur in April and May and the short rains in November and December, but you needn't worry about the terms as in both seasons there is never rain all day, and any storm is usually followed or preceded by a clear sunny spell.

Clothing

Be sensible about not wearing too much in the heat, but take enough along for the cooler moments. Dress is generally informal and there are unlikely to be occasions on the normal holiday when you will require anything formal. For men a blazer and trousers should be the most formal attire needed. For women loose, cool clothes are required for daytime wear, and for the evenings similar clothing to that worn on a good English summer's evening, with the option of something a little warmer for later on.

On safari you shouldn't be too influenced by the traditional image of the hunter in khaki shorts, short-sleeved khaki shirt and sun hat. The latter is about the most useful but long-sleeved shirts are preferable – they can be rolled down against the insects and to keep the sun from burning your arms. Trousers for the men and slacks for the women are the best option and shoes should be of the ankle-boot variety or gym shoes; certainly something sensible. Don't be too worried about the colours of your clothes as there is little evidence that animals can see colour, so bright red is unlikely to attract or frighten that elusive lion or leopard.

Food

Hotel food in Kenya is generally excellent, as there is an internationally recognised hotel school in Nairobi from where most of the hotels draw their staff. Cooking is basically English, with some international dishes also on the menu.

The great strength of Kenya is that it has excellent meats to draw on. The beef and lamb are particularly good, as is the bacon, which doesn't always look as good as it tastes. Most hotels have an ethnic

At the road side through the Great Rift Valley, where numerous local delicacies can be bought.

evening when the local African dishes are made for the tourists. Such vegetables as sweet potatoes and plantain bananas are cooked, but in general most tourists find them bland and a resistible treat second time around.

The fish is excellent with huge Nile perch often on the menu, or the tilapia or trout from the fresh water lakes and rivers. From the coast there is fish, prawns and lobsters.

Fruit is the real speciality of the country, with every imaginable exotic variety available. There are papayas (paw-paw), mango, giant avocado pears, pineapple, melons and bananas – all in abundant quantities. At breakfast there is always plenty of fresh fruit juice, although the orange looks distinctly anaemic by our standards. It also tastes lemony, but you soon get to love it.

With the Indian connection spicy food is becoming very popular and such snacks as vegetable or minced lamb samosas are widely available and make an excellent mid-morning break, washed down with a bottle of Kenyan beer.

Kenya is becoming quite cosmopolitan and eating out offers a wide variety of styles of cuisine – particularly in Nairobi and Mombasa. There is everything from Cantonese and Italian to the nouvelle cuisine style of cooking, although with more generous portions.

Drink

Beer is the staple drink of the country and, although being of the lager type, is very pleasant. There are several types: Tusker, White Cap, White Cap Export and Premium, with the last two being stronger and more expensive. All are brewed by Kenya Breweries and all prices are controlled by the Government, which means they are the same price in the restaurant or corner store as the Casino or Norfolk Hotel.

The same price control goes for soft drinks, which include the ubiquitous Coca Cola, Pepsi Cola and Fanta. They are sold in every corner of the country and are all quite safe to drink.

Spirits are generally very expensive – even the locally produced gin, vodka and scotch. Wine is becoming more popular and therefore slightly cheaper, although quality is variable. In a restaurant it costs from £10 a bottle, but in the shops can be bought for as little as £3 a bottle. There can be some surprising vintages and names available. I have come across a 1978 Margaux for a mere £10 on a restaurant wine list.

There are one or two individuals starting up their own vineyards up-country but they don't expect to be producing in any real quantity for a couple of years yet. Meanwhile they are making fruit wines, particularly papaya wine, which is improving all the time and is now quite drinkable.

Surprisingly the tap water is fine and drinkable in Nairobi and Mombasa; however, anywhere else it needs to be boiled or treated. If the water is suspect the hotel will leave a flask of cold boiled water in your room. In these circumstances avoid having ice cubes in your drinks as they are likely to made from the tap supply.

Health

Apart from being sensible about exposure to the sun there are a number of other precautions you should take.

Although it is not compulsory for a visitor to Kenya coming from Europe or the United States to have innoculations against cholera, typhoid and yellow fever, it would be unwise to go there without them. It is also worth checking whether you are up to date with your tetanus and polio. You should also consider a hepatitis jab, particularly if you are not going to stay on the tourist route and plan to strike out on your own. But, whatever else you decide on, you should always take malaria tablets. The newest and strongest ones are available through your doctor. Others can be obtained from the chemist. They are available locally too, but these days it is recommended that the course should start at least a week before you arrive in Kenya, and continue for a few weeks after. Check with your doctor for details.

If you do become ill there are plenty of doctors, or you can go to one of the hospitals – usually run by Europeans – who will always help. But prevention is always the best course, so be careful where you eat, drink and swim.

Inland lakes and rivers are unwise to take a dip in because of bilharzia – a nasty liver disease which is carried by water snails.

The flying doctor service is based at Wilson Airport, Nairobi, and although most tour operators are members, individuals may join for their period of stay for a very moderate sum.

Money

The basic unit of currency is the shilling. The shilling is then divided into 100 cents. Don't be tempted to trade on the black market as the

At Easter time the whole country is enveloped in Safari fever. The event is probably the toughest rally in the world, attracting the finest international drivers who often have to contend with some of the worst local drivers in the world.

penalties are severe, and the tricks of the black marketeers are numerous.

Banking hours are from 9 a.m. to 2 p.m., Monday to Friday, and some banks are open from 9 a.m. to 11 a.m. on the first and last Saturday of each month. Branches of banks at Jomo Kenyatta International Airport, Nairobi, usually run a 24-hour service. There are now also a number of Bureaux de Change which are open till much later in the afternoon. It is also possible to change money in hotels, but the rate is generally inferior.

It is illegal to enter or leave Kenya with any Kenyan currency and visitors should exchange surplus local currency before departure. On entering the country the visitor has to fill in a currency declaration form stating the type of currency and the form it's in (e.g. notes or

You have been warned!

travellers cheques), and every currency transaction has to be recorded on the form. The form is handed in before you leave the country. There is no limit to the amount of foreign currency imported into the country, and any unspent may be taken out.

Visa, American Express and Diners Club are the main acceptable credit cards.

Tipping is customary from the airport to the hotel, to the lodges, the drivers, waiters, car park attendants and back to the airport again. Don't overdo it though – a little frequently is the best bet, particularly with the hotel staff. Five to ten per cent of bills is about right. Wages in Kenya for non-skilled staff is low and tipping is an important supplement for most people.

Bargaining

You can bargain when buying items from the markets or street hawkers. Never pay the asking price and offer no more than 50 per cent at the outset. You will soon get a feel about prices and never be too embarrased to walk away from a sale and return later if that turns out to be the best buy.

Most shops don't bargain, although in some artefact shops they do. This is usually indicated by the seller saying he can do you a better price for something. You will have to use your judgement, although a rule of thumb is that the more expensive a shop, the less likely they are to entertain offers.

Hotels

In town hotels and lodges the check-out time is generally 10 a.m. and at most coastal hotels 11 a.m. If you need to stay longer ask the management, who will help if they can. If you are in transit then it is possible to book a room just for the day – usually up to 6 p.m. Many flights arrive in the early morning and most departures are at night. This does put pressure on rooms for early arrivals and if the room is essential it may be necessary to book for the preceding night.

Kenya's Ministry of Tourism and Wildlife is currently (1986) undertaking a grading of all hotels. When completed it will provide a complete reference system for quality and pricing. The classifications will be based on the size and fittings of the room, the extent of the services, the quality of the food and recreational facilities and the hotel's location. For example, a five star hotel will include colour TV and mini-bar in its rooms, whereas a four star hotel might only offer one of these. A three star might limit its hours of service to 16 hours a day and offer smaller rooms, but would probably provide a room telephone and bar service for the guests. It is unlikely that tourists will be offered lower graded hotels than these.

Security

In keeping with many tourist centres worldwide, visitors are advised to make use of the safe deposit boxes which are available at most hotels and lodges. Visitors should never carry large sums of cash and women are advised to keep a tight grip on handbags in crowds and busy streets. Avoid backstreets at night and, if possible, avoid walking at night altogether; use taxis or hire cars.

Numerous small aircraft ply the airways between the game parks and towns.

Telephones and Telex

There is now a modern telephone system in Kenya with direct dialling to most parts of the world, although it is not cheap. There are also excellent internal and external telex services which operate 24 hours a day. Radio call equipment is available at most lodges and tented camps in the remoter areas.

Public Holidays

January 1, Good Friday and Easter Monday, May 1, June 1 (Madaraka Day – the anniversary of self government), October 20 (Kenyatta Day), December 12 (Independence Day), December 25,

December 26. The Muslim festival of Idd-Ul-Fitr, which marks the end of Ramadan, is also a public holiday, as is Id-Ul-Azhar – the start of the pilgrimage to Mecca 70 days after the end of Ramadan. The dates are variable and the first is celebrated as a public holiday, while the second is a solely Muslim holiday.

Time

Kenya is three hours ahead of G.M.T., so at noon in England it is 3 p.m. in Kenya. It follows then that Kenya is only two hours ahead of British summer time.

Government and office business hours are from 8.30 a.m. to 12.30 p.m. and from 2 p.m. to 5 p.m. Shops open at the same time, closing from 1 p.m. to 2 p.m. for lunch if at all, and staying open to 5 p.m. at least; they are often open to around 7 p.m.

Bars open at 11 a.m. and close around 2 p.m., opening again from 5 p.m. to 11 p.m.

Electricity

The voltage is 240 volt A.C. and plugs are either two-pin or three-pin or three-pin square, so it is advisable to take an adaptor with you. The lights are the normal bayonet type.

5 The Animals

Its animals must be regarded as Kenya's most valuable asset, a fact recognised by the number of game parks throughout the country, and they are usually the main reason why tourists are attracted to this part of East Africa.

I have dealt here with just 31 of the main types of animal, small and large, that one can see on a trip, either without too much trouble, like the wildebeest, giraffe or zebra, or with a little luck and patience, like the lion. Leopard, on the other hand, are not often seen by the tourist. Animals such as the aardvark, which are generally nocturnal, are extremely difficult to locate, and even people who have lived in East Africa for years have never seen them; however, I have known tourists who have been there just a few hours and have spotted one, so don't give up hope!

Most visitors are driven round the parks by guides and will have many of the animals pointed out to them, but if you are on your own for the first time then a few tips are necessary. The first thing to remember is that these are wild animals, and no matter how strong the temptation is to get out of the car, *don't*. While you are in a vehicle the animals do not recognise you, and you are able to approach quite close, but your sudden appearance outside a car might well surprise and frighten them, and you could be attacked.

In the search for animals it is usually difficult to find them during the middle of the day, when the sun is at its hottest. The most rewarding period is early in the morning, when it is cooler and most animals are searching for their breakfast. An alternative time is at dusk which, because Kenya straddles the Equator, is short. Once the sun starts going down it is generally down within an hour.

The majestic giraffe silhouetted in the evening sunshine with another of Kenya's distinctive landmarks, the acacia tree.

Animal photography

Evening is the best time to see the bigger animals such as lion, cheetah and leopard, but photography is more difficult. Despite all the advice of a bright sun requiring a slow film, it is important to have faster films with you. I would suggest that you take along mostly 200 ASA films, a couple of 400 ASA and a few 64 ASA ones for the midday and coastal shots. In the parks you will need a range of camera lenses; in a car you can often approach an animal to within a few yards, and a standard lens might suffice, but you can't bank on it, so take a good telephoto lens with you. In general the instamatics and auto-focusing cameras will prove disappointing; there is no substitute for a good, SLR camera.

Don't drive too quickly through the parks as you can easily miss something. It is surprising how easily a cheetah can hide in short grass, or a giraffe behind a tree. Always have a good pair of binoculars with you as the parks are larger than you imagine and you will need them to look for animals in the distance.

Learn to recognise the tell-tale signs of a kill – the vultures circling in the air, or more likely sitting in a nearby tree waiting their turn to go in and clean up a carcass. Other animals, mostly hyenas, may also be agitatedly prancing about. Excited monkeys or baboons often mean the presence of some such animal as a leopard, so have a good look round before moving off.

Perhaps the biggest giveaway of all is the safari vans. They are in radio contact with each other, so when one finds something of interest, it doesn't take long for the others to come onto the scene. This is where your binoculars will come in useful, scanning the distance for the twinkle of car windows in the sunlight.

Finally, you should ask at the gate when you enter the park to find out whether the animal you wish to see has been spotted recently. The continuing welfare of the parks is based on satisfied customers so the wardens are only too happy to help out if they can.

Much of the land in game reserves is savannah, a rich pasture shaded with small trees, and it is here that you will see herds of different antelope. There are no territorial disputes and they all appear to live in harmony – several species can be grazing the same stretch of land, each eating different grasses and herbs. Antelopes come large and small, from the huge eland bulls weighing as much as 760 kg (about three-quarters of a ton) to the dainty dik-dik, which weighs on average a mere 4 kg (about 8 lb).

Wildebeest, which are easily the most numerous animal, generally share their grazing with zebra, and are naturally gregarious. Other antelopes, such as the duiker, are rarely found in any numbers, and are almost always solitary or in pairs. The duiker is among the species of antelopes which inhabit the patches of thick cover on the savannah, and has evolved shorter forefeet that make it easier to dive for cover – duiker means diver in Afrikaans.

Where there are antelopes there are also carnivores – lion, leopard, cheetah, hyena and wild dog – but if you expect to see a kill then you are liable to be disappointed. Of these only the cheetah generally kills during the daylight hours, when its speed can be used to the full. Lion and leopard as well as other smaller carnivores, such as the jackal, several cat and genet, are night time or early morning killers.

Elephant can be seen in most areas, ranging from the hot coastland to the Aberdares and Mount Kenya. They are in most parks, but if you wish to see them in herds of 100 or more you have to go to Tsavo park. They are on the move night and day foraging for 110–140 kg (250–300 lb) of food a day, causing great destruction wherever they go. It is easy to spot an elephant thoroughfare by the ravaged look to the trees and undergrowth.

The rhino is one of the most exciting animals to see, partly because it has become so rare following its wanton destruction for its horns, which are still considered in some countries to have aphrodisiac qualities, and partly because of the its character. It is unpredictable, but unless with young will rarely take much notice of you. The best time to see one is in the early morning as they get too hot later in the day.

The hippo is another of the large animals which is a real pleasure to find. However docile they may be in the water, when on dry land they can be extremely unpleasant, and lodges such as the Lake Baringo Club, owned by Block Hotels, the largest group in Kenya, has signs which warn the unwary tourist to keep an eye out for grazing hippos.

Crocodile are also found at Lake Baringo, but if you really want to see them in large concentrations then Lake Turkana in the north is where you should be. Another dangerous – some say the most danger-ous – animal, the buffalo, can be found just about everywhere, and although it may give you a steely stare it rarely charges. In herds they seem to be remarkably timid.

Whatever you do, remember that the animals are wild, and although they are in parks they are not tame and have learned through the ages that man is their major enemy.

Aardvark

Description
Aardvark means earth pig in Dutch; just to be confusing, this animal is often called the antbear, although to my mind it looks like neither. However, it does have bear-like arms and claws for digging while its bulky body slopes down into a kangaroo-like tale. The body is about 1.5 m (4–4½ ft) long and the tail is up to a further 60 cm (2 ft), and it can weigh around 70 kg (150 lb). It has long pointed ears, a narrow head and a snout, and the adults have long brown fur.

Habits
It is rarely seen by day, although found in all the game parks in Kenya. It feeds on termites, which in turn feed on everything else

remotely edible, but usually wood in some form. The aardvark has a
45 cm (18 in) tongue for the purpose. It can dig holes at a prodigious
rate, both when it is after a few ants or termites, but also when it is
frightened. A single offspring at a time is born in a burrow, and its
main enemies are lions and other large carnivores.

Aardwolf

Description

Aardwolf means earth wolf, and as you might expect it gets its name from living underground in burrows. It is quite small, being no more than 50 cm (20 in) high at the shoulder and looks like a small striped hyena. Its coat is a pale red-brown colour with vertical brown stripes on its side and horizontal stripes on its forelegs. There is a mane of brown hairs with black tips along its back, and the front of its face is black. Its length from nose to end of tail is about 90 cm (3 ft) in the adult.

Habits

It inhabits scrubby bush country and can be found in the Nairobi and Tsavo national parks. During the day it rests underground in small groups. It has small teeth and feeds on insects, including termites and beetles, as well as small mammals such as gerbils. When attacked it emits a vile smelling liquid from its anal glands.

Baboon

Description

The largest of the monkeys you will see, although there are two distinct species. The Neumann's olive baboon has a shaggy coat, thick mane over shoulders and cheeks and is olive grey all over. The yellow baboon is more slender, is a similar olive brown above, but is lighter elsewhere, particularly on its cheeks. It has comparatively short hair and little evidence of a mane. They are about 90 cm (3 ft) long, with tails another 45 cm (18 in).

Habits

Both types are found in the national parks although not always in the same ones. For instance the olive baboon is the only one found in the Nairobi park while the yellow baboon is common in Amboseli and Tsavo. Contrary to common belief, the baboon spends most of its time on the ground and not in the trees. It likes rocky areas where it is at a distinct advantage over most other animals. The adult is moody and unpredictable and can be extremely dangerous if thwarted or alarmed. It is very unwise to fall into the trap of feeding one, as when the food has run out it may attack you. The baboon usually eats grubs, spiders, scorpions, fruit, roots, insects and eggs.

Bat-eared Fox

Description

This most attractive little animal has enormous oval ears and is easily distinguishable from other foxes or dogs. It is quite small, being about 60 cm (2 ft) in length and can weigh up to only 4 kg (9 lb). It appears greyish in colour although it has some brown underlying fur, with a black face, legs and tip of brush.

Habits

Although primarily a nocturnal animal it can easily be seen in the early evening when it comes out of its burrow and lies around the entrance soaking up the failing sunshine. It spends the rest of the day below ground in its cool burrow. The staple diet is insects, but it is not averse to such little animals as mice and gerbils, or other meaty things as ground-nesting birds and lizards. An alternative diet is tuberous roots and wild fruits.

Buffalo

Description
It is not easy to confuse the buffalo with any other animal. It is large, black and similar to cattle but with huge downward-shaped horns which then curl up. It is very bulky and a bull can stand 1.5 m (5 ft) at the shoulders, weight around 800 kg (1800 lb) and have horns that span 127 cm (50 in). Of the big five (elephant, lion, leopard, buffalo and rhino) it is the easiest to see – and the most dangerous.

Habits

Although it mostly eats grass, in some areas it has been forced by encroaching civilisation to live in forests and thick bush. It is usually fairly docile in herds but when alone can be extremely dangerous. It has reasonable eyesight and charges with its head up and cannot be stopped by anything other than a bullet. Its only natural enemy are lions, but even they only attack with caution. If possible they will go for a calf, cow or a single older bull, and the lions do sometimes come off worst. The buffalo is a wallowing animal and likes nothing better than a muddy pool.

Cheetah

Description

A scaled-down leopard, with its spots scattered about singly rather than in groups. It stands 76–90 cm (2 ft 6 in–3 ft) high and can be up to 2.18 m (7 ft) in length. It is generally much lighter looking, with a smaller head than the leopard. It is hollow backed and carries its head low when it walks. The tail is ringed at the end with a white tip.

Habits

It is not an aggressive animal, not strictly a member of the cat family as it can't retract its claws, and can be very successfully tamed.

In the wild, because of its phenomenal speed – up to 112 kph (60 mph) – it hunts during daylight in open country. Sometimes a

pair will hunt together to trap a small but spritely antelope such as a
dik-dik. Although it has this great speed advantage it lacks stamina,
and if the prey is not within grasp after about 100 metres it will give
up. It growls when in a tight spot, but generally makes tweeting
noises rather like a bird, and purrs loudly when happy.

Colobus Monkey

Description
The most beautiful of the African monkeys. Fairly large, around
76 cm (30 in) for the body and a further 100 cm (40 in) for the tail, it
is black with long white fur flowing from its flanks and a long, white
bushy tail.

Habits
It hardly ever comes down from the trees, living off leaves and
finding water in hollows in trees. It only inhabits heavily-forested
areas and can be seen in the mountain parks of Mount Kenya and the
Aberdares. Entirely harmless and one of the real charmers of the
forest.

Crocodile

Description
This fellow needs no introduction, with its beady eyes and large jaw
which it often leaves open for an airing.

Habits
It is widely distributed in Kenya; generally, where there is a lake
there are crocodiles. It is surprisingly timid and if basking will waddle
towards the water's edge and disappear from view as you approach.
It generally eats fish, but if a tasty gazelle or some other such small
animal is unwise enough to come close to it, the crocodile will knock it
into the water with its tail and hold it down until it drowns. The
unfortunate animal is then usually hidden in some river bank until
high before it is eaten.

Dik-dik

Description

A small antelope standing around 40 cm (15 in) high at the shoulder, and weighing no more than a maximum of 6 kg (12 lb). It has a shaggy, dull, grey/brown coat but has a distinctive long nose. Horns are only seen on males. Be careful not to confuse it with the klipspringer which is similar but taller, standing around 50 cm (20 in) high at the shoulder.

Habits

It lives in dry thorn scrub and is generally only seen in pairs or singly. It is reputed not to need much water, hence its ability to live in the driest areas. This also means it is fairly common in all the game parks of Kenya, although it does tend to keep in the shade during the hotter periods of the day.

Eland

Description

It is the largest of the antelopes, and looks surprisingly like the Brahmin cattle of India – both have a fleshy dewlap hanging from the neck. Both sexes have horns twisted at the base and they are generally a greyish brown with light vertical stripes. It is a very big animal and can stand up to 2 m (6 ft) high to the top of the hump on its shoulder. A bull can weigh upwards of 760 kg (three-quarters of a ton) and can be nearly 3.5 m (11 ft) long, the length of a small car.

Habits

It is seen in most parts of Kenya, but probably the best examples are to be found around Nairobi and the Voi area near Tsavo. It is a browsing animal, liking leaves, fruits, young grass and shoots. It is migratory, but this migration is not connected with the search for

1 The lion looks peaceful, but make sure you keep your distance.

2 The world's fastest runner, the cheetah, as beautiful at rest as it is on the move.

3 Pink flamingos seen at Lake Nakuru.

4 Not many people's idea of a nice place to rest, but this vervet monkey doesn't seem to notice the thorns.

water, as with most migrations, but some other, ancient inner need. It is very mild tempered and even when wounded has not been known to charge. It congregates in herds – sometimes very large and often alongside giraffe and zebra.

Elephant

Description

Elephants don't need much description, but the African elephant is larger than its Indian cousin and also has larger ears. A full grown bull can weigh 6 tons and can stand up to 3.65 in (12 ft) at the shoulder. The African elephant also has much larger tusks and they appear on both sexes. The heaviest recorded weight for a tusk is 116 kg (235 lb), while the greatest recorded length is 3.5 m (11 ft 6 in). Their natural lifespan is about sixty years. Locally the elephant is called *tembo*, which also means beer, and I suppose that is the reason why the local brew is named Tusker!

Habits

It is extremely destructive, knocking over trees to reach the roots, which it eats. It also likes bark, seed pods, the flesh surounding palm nuts, wild fruits, tender shoots and grass. It is an important supplier of water for other animals, as the elephant will find a suitable spot, usually in a river bed, dig away the sand, and then stand in the hole and wait for the water to percolate up. It is known for being irritable and unpredictable. While a charging elephant can reach 40 kph (25 mph), it can't keep that up for long. It generally walks at around 6–8 kph (4–5 mph) in small groups or herds, and needless to say has no natural enemies except man. It is found in many of the game parks, although not in Nairobi. The Masai Mara and Amboseli are both excellent places for elephant watching.

Yes, they really do walk in a line, but I haven't seen them join trunk to tail yet.

Genet

Description

A cat-like creature with a long body, narrow, pointed face and large ears. It is about the size of a large cat but has a longer ringed tail and is easily distinguished by its colouring; a brown-grey coat covered with brown spots which tend to merge into stripes along the shoulders and back.

Habits

A nocturnal creature, although it can be spotted during the day stretched out along the branch of a tree. It is extremely carnivorous and enjoys eating anything it can kill – particularly chickens. It is also partial to such animals as hares, rabbits and roosting birds. It is easily domesticated and makes a good and beautiful pet.

Gerenuk

Description

This has the alternative title of giraffe-gazelle on account of its long neck and giraffe-like head. In fact it is quite distinctive from other gazelles and in all other respects looks nothing like a giraffe. It has a dark reddish-brown coat, slightly paler on the flanks and with white patches round its eyes. The exceptionally long neck is the most easily identified characteristic. The gerenuk is generally between 90 and 100 cm (35 and 41 in) tall and rarely weighs more than 45 kg (100 lb). Only the males have horns.

Habits

Usually found in small groups, although sometimes on its own or in pairs. It prefers the dry grass or thick thorn bush areas, which are often so dense that predators can't easily penetrate. It uses its long neck to reach high into the bushes for succulent shoots, or will stand up on its hind legs. The best time to see one is during the early morning or late afternoon, as during the hot period it will stay under cover.

Giraffe

Description

As impossible as it may seem, this distinctive animal is related to the hippo by virtue of having the same number of toes. That aside, there are two types – the common or Masai giraffe and the rarer reticulated variety. The Masai type has a rather untidy star-shaped chestnut pattern on a tan background. A bull can stand up to 5.5 m (18 ft) tall and weigh up to a tonne. The reticulated giraffe, on the other hand, which is found only in the Marsabit National Reserve, has a much more regular pattern of square shapes divided by white or light lines. It is a smaller animal too, standing between 4.5 and 5 m (15 and 17 ft) high. In both species the cows are 60–90 cm (2–3 ft) smaller but otherwise indistinguishable. They all have small horn-type extensions on their heads which are covered in skin and soft hair. One interesting aspect about the giraffe is that it has the same number of vertebrae in its long neck as humans (seven).

Habits

It is, of course, a browsing animal, using its long neck to reach the tasty younger shoots, mostly of the thorny acacia trees, which is its favourite food. It is an extremely gentle creature, with excellent

Giraffes don't always eat from the highest part of the tree.

eyesight, and will often stop eating to have a good look at you. The males occasionally fight by banging their necks together. However, if attacked the giraffe will defend itself with a kick like a pile driver. It does occasionally lie down, although its head will always remain erect.

Grant's Gazelle

Description

A gazelle is a species of antelope with slender legs, and in Kenya the Grant's gazelle is one of the two most common – the other being the

Thomson's gazelle. The most distinguishable feature of the Grant's is its graceful lyre-shaped horns which are carried by both the males and females. In proportion it is probably longer than any other African antelope. It is pale buff in colour with a white rump and underside, and a chestnut streak down the centre of its face. The female is similar, except for a darker stripe on her flanks. The male stands about 76 cm (30 in) at the shoulder and the female is slightly smaller. Adult weight varies from 68 to 73 kg (150 to 160 lb).

Habits
It lives mostly in the open plains and the acacia veld. It browses on leaves and shoots and eats grass. It associates in groups of from five or six, when there is a dominant male, to groups of thirty to forty.

Hartebeest

Description

The most common of the three types is Coke's hartebeest which has a long face with cupped horns. It is dark fawn in colour which fades towards a whitish rump. Fully grown it is around 1.2 m (4 ft) at the shoulder and weighs about 180 kg (300 lb). The sexes are similar in appearance, but the male's horns are generally larger.

Habits

As a grazing animal it stays mainly in the plains, although it is not
averse to the dry bush country. It congregates in herds, with lookouts
acting as sentries. It often grazes with other antelopes and zebras.
When frightened it is an extremely fast mover and it takes a good
horse to keep up with it. Although the hartebeest is still reasonably
common, it was at one time the most numerous of the antelopes.

Hippopotamus

Description

A member of the pig family by the toe-counting method, i.e. an even-toed ungulate. In Greek the name means 'horse of the river'. Most of the time all you will see of it are its eyes watching you from just above the surface of the water. Although it spends most of its time in the water it does go on land in the evening to graze. Here you can see the huge size of the beast. It can be up to 4.25 m (14 ft) long and 1.47 m (4 ft 10 in) high and weigh anything up to a massive 5 tons. Surprisingly, despite the short stubby legs, it can run faster than a man. It has four large curved tusks with two projecting from the front corners of the jaw and two others from the centre.

Habits

Although it spends a great deal of time under water it has to rise to the surface every four minutes or so to breathe. It is particularly good at keeping the vegetation down in rivers and lakes, helping to keep the water flowing. It is generally good-natured but when annoyed the male hippo can be a dangerous opponent; when two start fighting it is sometimes to the death. It is often thought to be dangerous to come between a hippo and the water, although this may not be strictly true.

Hyena

Description

A large dog-like creature with a sloping back, large jaws, rounded ears and a thick neck. It has a stubby mane on a reddish-grey body with a short bushy tail. As you would expect, the spotted hyena is covered in dark spots while the less common striped hyena has a striped coat. I will only deal with the spotted variety as it is quite common in the tourist areas. It usually stands between 76 and 90 cm (2 ft 6 in and 3 ft) high and is about 1.5 m (5 ft) in length. Its large jaws are some of the most powerful and can break a bone and chew it without any problem. It is not unknown for a hyena to bite the side off a man's face while he sleeps – fortunately though, this is not at all common.

Habits

Yes, it really does appear to laugh, but it is not because it has a sense of humour but because there is a lion in the vicinity. It has the reputation of being a scavenger, and so it often is, but it also kills for itself, usually old, lame or young animals. In fact, its kill is often

The hyena is a feared and necessary link in the wildlife chain.

taken away from it by lions, which appear to despise the hyena, probably because the hyena will kill them when they are old. It does have the nasty habit of eating its kill alive. It is usually a solitary animal or will hunt in pairs, but once a kill has been made they will all join in. It is mostly a nocturnal creature but can often be seen in the late afternoon or early morning; however, you are more likely to hear it howling than to see it.

Impala

Description

A medium-sized and most graceful antelope. It is reddish/brown and fawn with white underparts and black and white markings on rump and tail. It also has black tufts of fur sprouting just above the heel on the back legs. It has a characteristic white mark on either side of the rump below the tail, framed by black lines. Only the males have

An impala, monarch of the bush, surveys all before it in the stillness of the evening.

horns, which are curved in a wide lyre shape and can be up to 76 cm (30 in) long. The height of the impala is 89–97 cm (35–38 in) at the shoulder.

Habits

A widely-distributed animal, its main claim to fame being the ability to leap 9 m (30 ft) in one bound and jump 3 m (10 ft) in the air. When a whole herd are at it it's like looking at rolling waves. It is a better jumper than the springbok and usually takes off when frightened. During the rutting season the rams spend most of the time trying to get headaches by butting each other. It is a browsing animal but does not like water-less areas. It can be found in the scrub bush or thorny areas.

Jackal

Description

The jackal is a dog and is thought to be the ancestor of all domestic dogs. It looks much like a dog although the head appears a little like that of a fox. The common jackal in Kenya is the silver-backed, which has a saddle of silver hairs along its back while its flanks, head and legs are reddish-brown with some sandy coloured hair. Its tail is slightly bushy and has a black tip. Often the inner parts of its legs and stomach are very light.

Habits

An animal whose howl is bigger than its bite. It scavenges, getting most of its food as leftovers from a lion's feast, although it will kill smaller mammals and eat fruits and berries. It is quite cunning and will hunt in pairs, one luring an adult away from a newborn which the other will kill, but it prefers not having to work for its food. It is mainly nocturnal but if there is food about it will go for it, whatever the time of day or night.

Leopard

Description

A powerfully-built cat looking something like a cross between a lion and a cheetah. It stands 66–76 cm (26–30 in) high and weighs in at about 54 kg (120 lb). It is very spotty indeed, even along the tail, thick set and muscular, with a golden-coloured coat under the spots, and a light-coloured chest, throat and underbody.

Habits

A solitary animal with its own hunting range, it is rarely seen in action during the day, although it can be spotted relaxing on a shady tree branch watching the world go by. It is a nocturnal hunter and prefers the stealthy approach, rather than the chase like the cheetah, so it likes the thick bush or forests. It rarely remains in an area for very long, but wanders round its range in a nomadic manner. The staple diet is the small and medium-sized antelopes, although it is rather partial to the taste of baboons, monkeys, bushpigs and dogs. It will drop down from trees to kill its prey, then drag it back up to keep the carcass away from hyenas and lions. A very dangerous animal, it is not to be cornered as it will fight back ferociously. It is actually well-distributed around Kenya, but because of its liking for night and good cover is often the most dificult of the big five to find.

Lion

Description

Extremely imposing and one of the most exciting to see for the first time. They are very large and a fully-grown male will weigh up to 225 kg (500 lb). Most males have the famous mane although some have a very small one, however, all males will have some sort of beard which distinguishes them from the lionesses. The male is bigger and heavier than the female and can stand 107 cm (3 ft 6 in) at the shoulder and be 2.75 m (9 ft) long. There are records of them (mostly man-eaters) exceeding 3.35 m (11 ft) in length.

Habits

The King of the Beasts is surprisingly lazy and, like most hunters, prefers the night or the cool of the evening or morning for hunting, spending much of the day in a shady spot – though not usually well concealed. This makes it easy prey for the tourist, who can count himself very unlucky if he doesn't see a lion on a trip to Kenya. The male does much of the initial tracking and even selection of the prey,

but the lioness does the actual killing, it being impossible for a male with a large mane to move fast enough. The lion lives in the plains and will eat most animals; its prey is usually antelope and zebra, although it will hunt down ostrich and the occasional buffalo. If it is really hungry any animal will do – even man, which is why it is so dangerous to be in the open when a lion is about. It is also extremely protective of its young, and while it wouldn't mind one of its youngsters sniffing around a car, if a person were to get out of the car to get a closer look they would be in grave danger from an adult lion.

Oryx

Description
A distinctive antelope having long straight horns which are often longer in the female. It is a reddish-grey in colour with a striking black and white marked face. It also has a black band round its

foreleg, and the belly is usually white. It stands about 1.2 m (4 ft) high at the shoulder.

Habits

Said to be the least dependent on water of all the antelopes, it is often found in the driest parts. It is quite a sociable animal and goes around in large herds. It is a ferocious fighter – mostly with other oryxes, but the long horns are handy for impaling an unwary lion. The tough hides make good African fighting shields.

Rhinoceros

Description

A huge animal with a belly that can be as much as 3 m (10 ft) round. Its height is around 1.7 m (5 ft 6 in), length 3.35 m (11 ft) and it can weigh about two tons. It has a double horn which is actually a sort of

Grazing white rhino in the Meru game park.

5 Masai girls standing outside a traditional loaf-shaped mud house.

6 The beautiful jacaranda tree in bloom.

7. Who would have thought this gorgeous bird was a starling?

8. The goliath heron, magnificent in its flight, haunts the lakes of the Great Rift Valley.

close-packed hair, said to be an aphrodisiac; there is therefore a great and largely illegal trade in horns. There are two types in Kenya: the black rhino, which is more common, and the white rhino, which isn't white at all but gets its name from the Afrikaans word *wit* which means wide – a reference to its square jaw.

Habits

It is a herbivorous browsing animal, eating grass, thorny twigs and shoots, feeding mostly at night or in the cooler periods of the day, spending the hotter time in the shade. It has notoriously bad eyesight and probably can't see more than 15 m (50 ft) in front of itself, but to compensate has acute hearing and a fine sense of smell. If disturbed it will stand still, or snort and face the direction of the danger. Occasionally it will charge but this is generally more in hope than any expectation of actually finding its target! They are temperamental animals, even with their own sort, so don't expect any favours from them, particularly when they have young in tow.

Serval Cat

Description

Looks something like a small cross between a lynx and a leopard. It is about 50 cm (20 in) at the shoulder, has strong rear haunches, a small face, large ears and a short tail. Its coat is generally a light yellowish-brown with large black spots dabbed on in lines along the back. There are some black examples to be found but they are rare. Length of an adult is usually about 1.25 m (50 in) and it can weigh in at around 16 kg (35 lb).

Habits

A lover of marshy and wet areas, river banks and water holes. Remains hidden in the long grasses, hunting at night for its favourite meal of guinea fowl, small birds, cane rats and small antelopes. Has a call which sounds like 'how, how, how'.

Thomson's Gazelle

Description

At a glance it can easily be mistaken for a Grant's gazelle, but on closer inspection the differences become obvious. It is smaller and its white belly is divided from the reddish brown of its upper parts by a dark stripe across its side. On its rear it has a white area bordered by a dark line. It has a short twitching tail and both sexes have horns, although on the female they tend to be small, and sometimes twisted.

Habits

A widely distributed antelope, it is often seen on the plains in large herds. It is fairly tame although when alarmed will usually start stotting – a straight-legged form of jumping. Staple diet for a lot of the carnivores including jackal, leopard and lion.

Vervet Monkey

Description

This is also known as the black-faced monkey and is the commonest of all the East African monkeys. It has a grey coat, black face and white tufts on its cheeks. It has a long, black-tipped tail, and the scrotum of the male is bright blue. The total length of an adult is around 1.37 m (4 ft 6 in) with the tail accounting for around 60 cm (2 ft).

Vervet monkeys are among the friendliest of the wild animals but are fonder of each other's fleas.

Habits

Although widely found in the parks and scrub areas, it is not a forest animal. A very attractive monkey it is often quite tame and allows you to approach quite close. It has also become an excellent thief, so keep hold of smaller items – particularly food. When there is a leopard about it will chatter and mob him, revealing his existence to each other – and you. It is often found along the banks of streams and rivers, where it feeds on fruits, grubs, birds' eggs and the gum of the acacia tree.

Waterbuck

Warthog

Description
A wild pig with large tusks protruding from either side of the face, and a tail which stands up when it is running about. It derives its name from the large warts which decorate its ugly head. Apart from a mane of a few bristles it has no coat. It is quite large, standing about 76 cm (30 in) high, weighs around 82 kg (180 lb) and is about 90 cm (3 ft) in length.

Habits
Apart from the tails the other peculiarity is to kneel on its front legs while digging with its snout for roots or drinking. It is normally seen in families although it will gather in larger groups where there is a good wallowing hole.

Waterbuck

Description
Kind-faced and thick set antelope with a wiry coat, grey-brown in colour, the common species having a white ring around its rump. The Kenyan Defassa species has a white patch on the inner sides of its rump instead. It has a white ruff round the throat and white marks over the eyes. Only the males have horns, which curve gently upwards and backwards up to a length of around 64 cm (25 in). It stands about 130 cm (50 in) at the shoulder and weighs around 180 kg (400 lb).

Habits
It is very widely spread, being a gregarious herding animal, often to be seen with other species such as wildebeest, other antelope and zebra. It lives in the plains but generally does not wander far from water, and will not hesitate to take refuge in a river or waterhole if attacked.

Wildebeest

Description
Also known as the gnu, it is a rather silly-looking antelope, related to the hartebeest. It is hump-backed with cow-like spreading horns, a mane, a dark grey body and a white or light-coloured beard. It looks

a bit like an ox, stands about 1.5 m (5 ft) high at the shoulder and weighs about 250 kg (550 lb).

Habits

A herding animal, it is one of the most common antelopes in East Africa and inhabits the plains. It is basically a grass-eater but never strays far from water. When water gets short it will migrate, usually in vast herds which sweep across the plains. In the early morning it will spend some time at play, chasing other wildebeest and frolicking.

Zebra

Description

A distinctive animal, of which there are two types: the common and Grevy's. Grevy's has narrower, closer striping but is rare in Kenya. A stallion can stand up to 12 hands (1.3 m/4 ft 3 ins), weighs on average 272 kg (600 lb) and can be 2.4 m (8 ft) in length. It always manages to look plump and well-fed, no matter how hard the drought.

A classic pose for the zebra, that most African of animals.

Habits
This African horse is a plains animals which congregates in herds and is constantly on the move, although it never strays far from water. It migrates annually, often in herds of several hundred, in search of water and fresh grazing. It is not easily tamed, but it has been done.

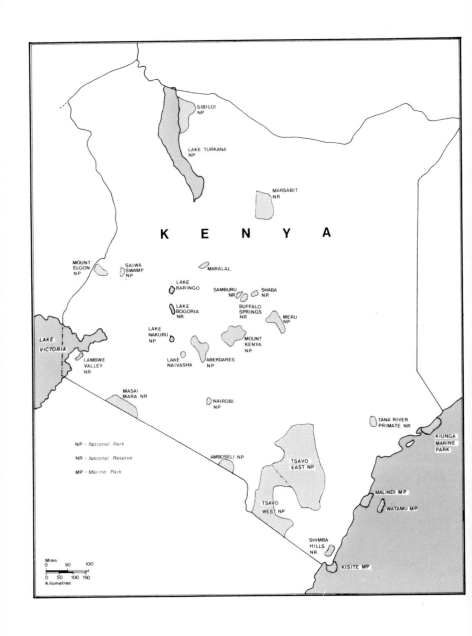

6 The Game Parks

Aberdares

The Aberdares is the now traditional name of a range of mountains which thrusts directly north from Nairobi for more than 100 miles. It was named after Lord Aberdare, then president of the Royal Geographical Society by that brilliant and much underestimated explorer, Joseph Thompson. He walked the range in 1883, getting to within ten miles of Mount Kenya before his presence was no longer tolerated by the Masai.

Part of the range is protected by the Aberdares National Park which encompasses all land over 3,200 m (10,500 ft) high, together with a small spur stretching east down to 200 m (7,000 ft) near Nyeri.

The park is a fairyland, awesome in its majesty and beauty, but crossing the range is an unpredictable event since rain is heavy and frequent. The highest point of the Aberdares is Ol Doinyo La Satima (Masai for mountain of the young bull) at 4,000 m (13,120 ft). Here in misty moorlands are strange 6 m (20 ft) tall mutants of alpine plants, Groundsel, Erica, Hypericum and Seneccio, whose brilliant yellow flowers bloom only once in 20 years. Icy rivers plunge in glorious cascades and enormous waterfalls. The eastern spur, which thrusts a dense forest through farming areas is where both The Ark and Treetops hotels are located. Once the spur was used as an elephant migration route but sadly that is no longer the case; however, it is rich in wildlife, particularly elephant and rhino. There are also plenty of warthog, giant forest hog and bush pig, waterbuck, duiker, dik-dik, eland and bushbuck, as well as the black and white colobus monkey which never leaves the trees.

The cats are here too, in the shape of the lion (it's a bit hairier here than in the plains), the leopard, genet and serval – the latter frequently being seen on the moorlands in its black (melanistic) coat.

In the Aberdares the termites seem to be able to build bigger than anywhere else.

Birds are not only plentiful but spectacular. The crowned eagle (which eats monkeys) is everywhere and the forest echoes to the cry of the silvery-cheeked hornbill.

Nyeri, the largest town in the Aberdares, is a longish drive from Nairobi although an easy one from Lake Naivasha, where many visitors spend a day or two. The Aberdares is a glorified landscape to be savoured and not rushed – but choose a fine day if you can.

To stay at Treetops, the most famous hotel in Kenya as well as the African continent, one goes to the Outspan Hotel at Nyeri first, lunches at 12.30 on the verandah overlooking the immaculate lawn, then takes the minibus to Treetops. There the intrepid overnighters are met by the hunter (usually in fact an ex-hunter) but who adds to the drama of the occasion by dire warnings about the animals and how one mustn't wander out of the hotel after dark. It's all good fun. Treetops itself is nestled into large Cape chestnut trees and stands on stilts. What you see before you is the second Treetops, the first having been burnt down by the Mau Mau in 1954 during their drive for independence. One of its claims to fame is that in February 1952 the then Princess Elizabeth became the successor to the throne of Britain while staying there, although she wasn't to know about it until she and Prince Philip were at Sagana State Lodge, the stay being a wedding gift to them from Kenya, a few days later.

The Ark is a luxurious look-out built in 1969 in the Treetops mould, and similarly has a staging post the Aberdare Country Club, a converted farm house. To reach The Ark there is a 370 m (1,200 ft) climb in just 18 km (11 miles) with the mandatory gun-toting hunter to give the occasion an authentic feel. Once there, though, there is excellent food, showers and a good panoramic view, as well as the obligatory hides for the photographers. Both The Ark and Treetops are built round watering holes and salt licks (natural or otherwise) which attract the animals.

The Outspan ('outspan' means to unyolk or unharness – particularly buffalo and cattle) is in Nyeri, a small township 1800 m (5,800 ft) above sea level and best known for being the burial place of Lord Baden-Powell, the founder of the scout movement.

Paxtu

Robert Stephenson Smyth Baden-Powell, the Hero of Mafeking and founder of the world Boy Scout and Girl Guide movements, did not visit East Africa, his final and chosen resting place, until 1906, although he had seen brilliant army service elsewhere on the African continent in 1884/5, 1888/9, 1895/6 and from 1899 to 1900.

After seeing Kenya he recorded his impressions in both words and pictures in his book, *Sketches in Mafeking and East Africa*, published in 1907. Three years later he devoted his full-time energies to the creation of the Boy Scout movement. By 1920 he was proclaimed Chief Scout of the World by the scouts gathered in London for the First World Jamboree.

Lord and Lady Baden-Powell returned to Kenya in 1935, when he carried out inspections of scouts at rallies organised throughout the country, and visited some friends at Nyeri. It was on that visit that Baden-Powell fell in love once again with 'the wonderful views over the plains to the bold snow peaks of Mount Kenya', to such an extent that when ordered by his doctor in England to rest in the winter of 1937, it was to Nyeri and The Outspan Hotel that he chose to come.

The Outspan cottage, Paxtu, was built specially for them and in October 1938 they came to the cottage, to remain there until the Chief Scout's death. Paxtu seemed to be the inevitable name for the cottage. The Baden-Powell's English home at Bentley, Hampshire, was called Pax Hill. Lord Baden-Powell wanted his little Outspan cottage to be called Pax too – Pax 2 or Paxtu. 'We are utterly and supremely happy here,' Lady Olave Baden-Powell wrote to her children in 1938.

Comprising a sitting room with a large verandah, two bedrooms, two bathrooms and two fireplaces, with its own private garden, Paxtu was an ideal place for B-P to write and sketch. Lord Baden-Powell died on 8 January 1941, almost 84 years old, and he is buried in Nyeri. In 1946 Kenya Scouts and Guides subscribed towards a memorial seat in the garden at Paxtu. Preserved now in his memory, Paxtu has been redecorated internally in the Scouts colours of blue and gold.

In July 1973 the 24th World Scout Conference, the first of its kind to be held in Africa, met in Kenya, when the third generation Lord Baden-Powell visited the Outspan and Paxtu as well as the Nyeri churchyard, the scene each February 22 (Scouts' Founders Day and Guides' Thinking Day) of pilgrimages of Scouts and Guides from all over the world. On his grave is the Scout trail sign, 'I have gone home.'

Mount Kenya

Mount Kenya is the country's highest mountain, reaching towards a snow-capped 5,199 m (17,058 ft) and sitting astride the equator. Everything above 3,200 m (10,500 ft) forms a national park.

In fact the mountain consists of three principal zones: the rocky peak area, actually an eroded volcanic plug, with its cloak of glaciers and snowfields; the alpine zone, with its distinctive giant vegetation; and the vast gentle slopes drenched in mountain forest and bamboo jungle.

Naro Moru River Lodge, the starting point for many an expedition to Mount Kenya.

Many rivers flow from the perpetual snows, among them the mighty Tana River, the source of much of the country's electricity supply.

Most visitors are content to marvel at the mountain's beauty but some will want to reach its summit, a feat requiring considerable rock-climbing skill. But the mountain's lesser peaks and glaciers can all be scaled and walked by the fit and adventurous. Point Lenana at

4985 m (16,355 ft) can easily be reached. There is a magnificent walk round the mountain from hut to hut which has almost perpetual breathtaking vistas.

Wildlife within the forest below the park boundary includes elephant, buffalo, lion, several species of antelope – including the rare bongo – and occasionally the dark-coloured leopard and serval cat. Much of the game can be seen from the safety of Mountain Lodge hotel, which lies just inside the forest on the south side of the mountain.

Mountain climbers should appreciate the need for acclimatisation over several days before attempting the high peak area. Naro Moru River Lodge specialises in assisting climbers with guides and porters and has all equipment necessary for a climb. It is also a beautiful place to stay for a few relaxing days. It is quite unwise to attempt to climb during the rains and the best times to go are January, February and late August to September. (Serious climbers should get in touch with the Mountain Club of Kenya, PO Box 45741, Nairobi).

For those who wish to savour the mountain air, the glorious views, peace and tranquility of the mountain, there are numerous hotels around the foothills, the most luxurious being the Mount Kenya Safari Club.

Amboseli National Park

The Amboseli National Park is at the foot of and in the shadow of Mount Kilimanjaro, the highest mountain in Africa at 5895 m (19,340 ft). On a fine day its snow-capped peaks provide the perfect backdrop for the photographer, but it is more likely to be at least partially covered by a ring of cloud. The best time to see it is soon after sunrise.

The park is large, around 3920 square kilometres (1513 square miles), and borders straight onto Tanzania. Years ago this was the area around which such famous writers as Ernest Hemingway spun their stories of big game hunters in the African wilds. It is also the homeland of the Masai people, the great proud warriors of Africa. They have learned to live in harmony with their surroundings and the wildlife. All round the borders of the park are occupied and abandoned manyattas – Masai villages. Built of bent poles and sticks and plastered with cow dung, they are quickly built and equally quickly abandoned when the grazing is finished and the herd must move on. The Masai have an agreement with the Kenyan Government to keep out of the park, but in times of drought they can be seen taking their cattle to the natural watering holes of the area.

The snows of Kilimanjaro also form a backdrop to one of Kenya's most spectacular displays of wildlife – lion, elephant, leopard, rhino, cheetah, buffalo and hosts of plains game which make the park a photographer's paradise. To see all the animals, including such rare ones as the gerenuk and serval cat, it is advisable to hire a guide who will know all out-of-the-way places wher these animals can be found.

Part of the park is composed of a dried up lake bed which in the shimmering heat produces mirages. Swamps and springs, fed by underground rivers from Kilimanjaro's melting snows, form permanent watering places for the wildlife in times of drought. The lake bed is subject to sporadic floods which dissolve noxious salts in the gravel beds and serve as a deadly poison for what is left of the local woods; few acacia trees, once a fine feature of this region, remain.

The park's popularity is also causing serious concern as tourist vehicles leaving the road are destroying its fragile, but ecologically precious, grassland. Park rules now insist that vehicles stick to the road and tracks, so don't encourage your driver to take to the open range.

Many attractive and semi-tame birds can be easily seen and photographed around the lodges. This is one of the few places where the rare and beautiful Taveta golden weaver is found. The park's best game runs are around the Enkongo Narok and Olkenya lake swamp, and there is a fine lookout point on Observation Hill which offers views over the whole of the park and beyond.

The best hotel in the best position in the park is the Amboseli Serena Lodge, which stands in the centre of the park within easy reach of the plains and swamps, and is built in the style of the traditional Masai manyatta. Nearby is the cheaper Kilimanjaro Safari Club, formerly a tented camp, and outside the park is the Kilimanjaro Buffalo Lodge, another first class hotel with relatively luxurious rondavels (round huts), a pool, good food and conference facilities. Another hotel worth considering is the Amboseli Lodge.

Lake Baringo and Bogoria

If you are a keen birdwatcher then this is the area for you. Lake Baringo is situated in a spectacular part of the Great Rift Valley about 280 km (175 miles) north of Nairobi. It is a haven of beauty and peace in an otherwise harsh but majestic landscape. There is an overwhelming sense of being at one with nature in all its scenic splendour.

Hippos and crocodile abound but most visitors are entranced by the multitude of birds. More than 400 species have been identified and the Goliath Heronry on a rocky islet (known locally as Gibraltar Rock) is world famous. Birdwatching is by boat or on foot, and other leisure activities include the possibility of a visit to a local Njemps village where traditional crafts and dancing can be seen.

Accommodation at the lake is either at the Baringo Island Camp or Lake Baringo Club, which has its own resident ornithologist who will take you on birdwatching tours, either along the lake or by the spectacular cliffs which form part of the Great Rift Valley. The Island Camp is sheer escapsim where you can not only take a trip to the heronry but indulge in water sports.

Lake Bogoria was hidden from the world for years because of its inaccessibility; travellers could pass by within a few miles and never even know it was there. Now there is a road leading to the lake which presents an exciting contrast to the more conventional game parks to the south and east. The lake and an area around it form a National Reserve, and although it is primarily scenic it is by no means devoid of wildlife. Hundreds of thousands of flamingos are to be seen as well as, on the north-eastern shore, the greater kudu. The journey along the shoreline is made more exciting by the boiling geysers and jet streams, showing the volcanic origins of the rift.

Lake Naivasha

Few lakes in the world have a more commanding or lovely setting than Lake Naivasha, the highest and purest of the Great Rift Valley lakes. It lies 84 km (52 miles) from Nairobi and is dominated by the shadow of the 2740 m (9000 ft) Mount Longonot, an extinct volcano.

Between Longonot and Naivasha lies Hell's Gate with challenging 300 m (1000 ft) rock climbs, and Fischer's Tower, a pinnacle of rock. Much game inhabits the area, including the rarest of Kenya's vulture population, the lammergeyer, which nests on the cliffs.

Lake Naivasha provides an idyllic aspect, its shores lined with flourishing farms, including newly developed vineyards and thousands of attractive yellow-barked acacia xanthophloea–Kipling's fever trees.

It is an ideal place for leisure pursuits which include birdwatching–more than 340 species can be spotted. Other activities are water skiing, fishing (the lake is well known for black bass and tilapia–a local speciality), adventure trekking and game watching. A private game sanctuary, Crescent Island, gives visitors the chance to walk among small herds of plains game, including waterbuck, dik-dik and Thomson's gazelles. The lake also has a resident herd of hippo.

The area around the lake is deeply associated with the history of the Massai's fight against the Arab slave trade caravans, which passed through the area after trips to the north, over the last three centuries. For a few months from 1949 it also served as the Nairobi terminal on the London-to-Cape Town flying boat service run by B.O.A.C. The cottages which passengers stayed in are still used by one of the lakeside hotels.

The lake shore was for many years the home of the late Joy Adamson. It was here that she raised her lioness Elsa, the heroine of the best selling book *Born Free*.

There is accommodation at Fisherman's Lodge, Lake Naivasha Hotel and Safariland Lodge

Lake Nakuru National Park

Lake Nakuru, a shallow and alkaline lake on the bed of the Great Rift Valley, has earned its fame as the home of the greatest bird spectacle in the world – a vast flock of more than a million pink flamingos which feed on the abundant algae which thrives in its shallow warm waters.

Nakuru is about 160 km (100 miles) north of Nairobi and the road passes by another famous flamingo lake, Lake Elementaita, but it is surrounded by private ranching land, making it difficult to gain access.

There is a road leading to Lake Nakuru National Park just after Gilgil which skirts Lake Elementaita and climbs a hill on the south-west side of Lake Nakuru to reveal a panoramic view of this fascinating reserve. The other route is through Nakuru town, now Kenya's fourth largest population centre and the farming capital of the country.

The lake is subject to fluctuations in depth of the water and once in every two or three decades it dries up completely. Then the vast flocks of flamingos and the pelicans use the rising morning thermals of the Rift Valley to gain enough lift to fly over the Menengai crater – the rim of an extinct volcano – and on down to the more remote waters of Lake Bogoria. Other less obvious inhabitants of Lake Nakuru include

Most tourists will be transported around Kenya in one of these minibuses.

black-winged stilts, avocets and, in the European winter, a mass of ruffs.

But it has a lot more to offer besides its magnificent bird lake, and there are also a few lions, an occasional leopard, buffalo and other plains and forest game which have made it their permanent and protected habitat. The acacia savannah which surrounds the lake is in itself beautiful and provides an area which is particularly delightful for game watching. There is accommodation at Lake Nakura Lodge and Lion Hill Camp.

Lake Turkana

The region around Lake Turkana has become famous in recent years as one of the great sources of evidence of modern man's roots. It lies roughly 640 km (400 miles) north of Nairobi by road, is 300 km (185 miles) long and is often known as the Jade Sea because of its colour.

This desert ocean was named Lake Rudolph by the first Europeans known to have set eyes on it, Count Teleki and Lt. Ludwig Von Hohnel of Austria, who reached its south-eastern shores early in 1888. The Kenyan Government changed its name to Lake Turkana in 1975.

It is one of the largest of the chain of lakes which lie along the floor of the Great Rift Valley. Fed by the Omo River which rises in Ethiopia, the 48 km (30 mile) wide delta at the north end of the lake forms the border with Kenya.

In this area, in the far north-east of Kenya, around the tiny settlements live one of the least known groups of people in the world – the semi-nomadic Merille who spread across the national borders of Kenya and Ethiopia.

The eastern shore of Lake Turkana, which is 60 km (36 miles) wide at its maximum, has been christened the Cradle of Mankind, and is the area in which the Leakey's made their discoveries (mentioned in Chapter 3). This tremendously rich fossil region has revealed numerous clues to the origins of modern man and some of his predecessors, dating back almost three million years. It has also provided an abundance of prehistoric animal fossils, including bones of an elephant which roamed these parts one-and-a-half million years ago.

Sibiloi National Park

A permanent museum has been established at Koobi Fora, a sand spit jutting into the lake just a few miles north of Alia Bay, which is the headquarters of Kenya's most remote national park, Sibiloi. The fossil excavations which lie within the park are clearly marked and must not be disturbed. One of the park's many features are giant tracts of petrified wood, remnants of the great forests which once lined these shores in primeval times.

Though extremely wind-blown and arid, the park has a surprising variety of wildlife, including Grevy's zebra, ostrich, gerenuk, oryx and the tiang – a unique sub-species of the topi antelope. The park's borders extend into the water of the lake, embracing some of Turkana's resident population of about 12,000 Nile crocodiles, the world's largest crocodile community, besides many hippo and a number of species of fish including the giant Nile perch.

Along these shores the Gabbra people tend their flocks of goat and camel herds. Noble and semitic looking, the Gabbra have one of the

most unified societies in Africa – a kinship which in the past streng-
thened and developed out of the need to protect the community
against the depredations of its voracious neighbouring tribes. Lake
Turkana is also world-renowned for its immense variety of bird
life – flamingo, waders, waterfowl, pelican and raptors all existing on
and around what has been described as an ornithological paradise.

Big-game fishing – species include the ferocious tiger fish, tilapia,
which makes excellent eating, and giant Nile perch which top the
scales at as much as 100 kg (220 lb) – is also a spectacular sport on the
lake's limpid waters, which can turn into a tempest in minutes when a
sudden gale blows and winds whip down from the crest 2164 m
(7100 ft) of Mount Kulal on the south-east shore.

The southern end of Turkana harbous an inferno known as Suguta
Valley, separated from the lake of which it was once a part by a
914 m (3000 ft) high volcanic mass, known as The Barrier. This is one
of the hottest places on earth, with noon temperatures averaging
between 54° and 60°C (130° and 140°F).

Suguta forms a natural and inhibiting demarcation between the
Samburu people, cousins of the better known Masai to the south, and
the warlike Turkana, who inhabit all the lake's western shores and
number more than 200,000. Feared by all their neighbours, and
equipped with a formidable arsenal of hand weapons including wrist
and finger knives, these remarkably hardy people are now being
assimilated into the framework of modern Kenya.

They are administered from the regional centre of Lodwar, which
lies about 56 km (35 miles) inland from the bulging midriff of Lake
Turkana and the sheltered haven of Ferguson's Gulf, a major base
for game fishing and also the departure point for excursions to the
biggest of Turkana's three islands, Central Island. The other two
islands are known, just as imaginatively, as South and North islands.
Only Central Island, a favourite breeding ground of the Nile
crocodile, has any form of semi-permanent population. The island
has three small lakes named Crocodile Lake, Flamingo Lake and
Tilapia Lake, the latter being a vivid green, a colour created by the
algae.

South Island is deserted apart from a flock of goats, while North
Island is noted for its resident population of some of the most
venomous snakes in the world.

Although thousands of years ago Turkana once served as a feeder
to the White Nile, it now has no outlet and the shoreline of this inland
sea is slowly receding as the harsh African sun sucks it dry, only
partially to be replenished by the Omo's seasonal floods.

Accommodation is available in the area of the lake at El Molo Camp, Oasis Lodge and Lake Turkana Fishing Lodge.

Lake Victoria and the Lambwe Valley

Lake Victoria is the world's second largest freshwater lake covering an area of 67,900 square kilometres (26,200 square miles) – about the size of the Republic of Ireland – and forms the main headwaters of the River Nile. It is about 354 km (220 miles) by road from Nairobi.

Three countries share the lake: Kenya, Tanzania and Uganda. In Kenya there is a busy network of waterways between the trading towns and villages which lie along the shores of the lake. Lighters and small cargo vessels ply daily from Kisumu down as far as the Tanzanian border, and north as far as Port Victoria near Uganda.

Kisumu, the capital of western Kenya and the country's third-largest population centre with more than 150,000 people, is the home of several industries and many small scale fisheries. Tilapia, Nile Perch and several other species provide a steady income for the fleets of Luo fishing canoes and boats which sell their catches at any of several markets located along the lake's coast. With their triangular sails these traditional dugout vessels provide an attractive sight.

Kisumu came into existence with the completion of the Uganda Railway five years after line laying began almost 1600 km (1000 miles) away in Mombasa. It was briefly called Port Florence after the wife of Ronald Preston, the line's railhead engineer. She had driven home the last bolt in the line in 1901. Only 40 years earlier, the English explorer John Speke, having travelled along the western side of the lake, reached a place named Ripon Falls. It was these cataracts, at what is now Jinja in Uganda, which he proclaimed as the source of the Nile in 1861.

The lake once had abundant hippo and crocodile but now these are much reduced. Halfway between Kisumu and Kendu Bay a small inland crater lake (Sindi) offers the spectacle of flamingo. There is also a famous heronry near Kisumu where as many as a thousand large and spectacular water birds can be observed breeding between March and July.

Homa Mountain, at 1751 m (5746 ft), marks the peninsula inside which is the small town of Homa Bay. From here it is possible to visit Rusinga Island, using a chain ferry, which is a burial place of one of Kenya's greatest statesmen, Tom Mboya. The island is also famous for the early remains of an early man-like ape which have been found there.

Lambwe Valley National Reserve, which is 81 km (19 miles) from Homa Bay, was established in 1966 primarily to protect roan antelope, of which there are a large number in the area. It is quite isolated and seldom visited.

You can get accommodation at Sunset Hotel, Kisumu, and Homa Bay Hotel.

Maralal

The frontier town of Maralal is the administrative headquarters of the Samburu people. A staging point for visitors to eastern Lake Turkana, it has a gem of a bird sanctuary within the township's boundaries. On the cedar-clad hillside and in the acacia scrubland below there is much resident game. Impala, eland, buffalo, baboon, warthog and zebra live in harmony but are ever watchful for leopard and hyena. Seasonally elephant visit the sanctuary, descending from the forested hills which lie to the north.

Much of the wildlife can be seen from the comfortable verandah of Maralal Safari Lodge, for the only permanent water in the sanctuary is a small waterhole just a few yards away. Here, throughout the day and at night by floodlight, is an almost continuous parade of wildlife. Leopard are enticed with food out of a small forest not far from the lodge and can be seen from a specially constructed hide.

The rocky track which leads north to Lake Turkana passes across the moorlands and forest of the Leroghi plateau, a seemingly boundless area of tranquil beauty. About 16 km (10 miles) from the town a dry weather track leads west across the plateau to the edge of the Great Rift Valley. Here at a place called Losiolo the wall of the Rift Valley is almost sheer and the vast panorama is stunning, and a little eerie in its loneliness.

In all directions from Maralal is majestic scenery whose grandeur is enhanced by the wildlife and the local people, with their herds of cattle. It is about as unspoilt a place as one can find on earth.

There is accommodation at Maralal Safari Lodge.

Marine National Parks

When they were introduced in 1968 the two marine national parks in Kenya, at Malindi and Watamu, were also the first in Africa. Since then two other parks have been added, Kiunga, north of Lamu, and Kisite-Mpunguti, near the Tanzanian border. Within the parks fish, shells and corals are entirely protected, although licensed local fishermen can operate within the reserves.

All four parks are within the fringing reef; the water is warm, and entirely safe for bathing. Within each park are extensive coral gardens whose beauty is overwhelming and which attract myriads of brightly-coloured coral fish. At Kiunga the most exciting coral formations centre on the tiny islet of Kiu, a fabulous haunt for the scuba enthusiast and reached by private boat from Kiwayuu Island. At Malindi the coral gardens are close to Casuarina Point, a few miles south of the town, and almost all hotels have daily boat runs to the best areas for snorkelling. For non-swimmers glass-bottomed boats hover above this underwater fairyland.

At Watamu the hotels also supply boats to visit the coral, which lies close to the entrance to Mida Creek. This entrance is narrow and guarded by giant grouper. These huge fish can reach a weight of several hundred kilos. Mida Creek is also a bird sanctuary, and between March and May hundreds of thousands of migrating waders are to be found. Perhaps the most beautiful marine park, both above and under the water, is Kisite-Mpunguti, reached from Shimoni. A small Lamu dhow has been tastefully converted for visitors to reach the park in style and comfort (and which returns to a sumptuous lunch on Wasini Island). The islet of Kisite is especially beautiful and is the nesting ground of the roseate tern.

The best time for snorkelling within the parks is for two hours on either side of low tide, when water movement least disturbs the bottom of the ocean and the coral gardens are near the surface.

Marsabit

Marsabit Mountain and the Chalbi Desert are two distinctive and unusual features in the far north of Kenya. Marsabit Mountain, about 560 km (350 miles) from Nairobi, was born of volcanic fire. It rises out of a vast and forbidding desert region, bounded on the north-west by the Chalbi Desert.

The peak, rising 1706 m (5598 ft) off the desert floor, has created its own ambient climate. Each evening around midnight the hot air rising from the desert cools and forms clinging fingers of mist which grasp the mountain top, rarely releasing it before early afternoon. Although the lower slopes of this 3402 square kilometre (1313 square mile) reserve are scorched and dry, the higher slopes form a richly-forested wonderland of crater lakes and swamps, towering cliffs and giant trees, with a dazzling array of wildlife. Here bird and beast live among tall juniper and yew.

Many species of birds of prey inhabit the shaggy cliffs and treetops around Paradise and Sokorte Guda, a cliff-lined bowl which forms a natural amphitheatre in which Marsabit's elephants parade to water in the late afternoon, mingling with large herds of buffalo. For an estimated 63 years Marsabit was the home of Ahmed, a mighty elephant protected from hunters who were after his huge tusks by a special Presidential decree. His skeleton and stuffed body can now be seen and marvelled at in the Nairobi Museum. Other species found on the mountain include antelope such as the greater kudu as well as leopard and lion.

Lower down the mountain, below the forest line, groups of the Borana people drive their camels to water at the singing wells. Three or four men form a human ladder down these deep shafts and with camel-hide buckets work in swift relay to feed the water into troughs. The songs they sing have earned the wells their name.

Marsabit is the staging post from which to venture into the inhospitable Chalbi Desert. This shimmering stretch of sand continues for almost 306 km (190 miles) to the shore of Lake Turkana, of which it was once a part. Even today, perhaps once in a decade in one of the torrential downpours which occur during a rare rainy season, it will again come into flood to form a vast but shallow lake.

For accommodation try the Marsabit Lodge.

Masai Mara National Reserve

Set at an altitude of 1588 m (5210 ft) the rolling grasslands of the Masai Mara offer one of nature's most dramatic spectacles – the annual migration of more than a million wildebeest and zebra from Tanzania's Serengeti, which takes place from late July to September.

The journey to the Masai Mara, which lies 275 km (170 miles) west of Nairobi, can be made by air, with expansive panoramic views of the floor of the Great Rift Valley, including the so-called lost world volcano of Suswa with its inner plateau, or by road, along the south slopes of the Mau, which is scenically magnificent. On the road, after Narok, the journey becomes a rough, testing experience through grey alluvial dust and the jolting of marram and rock roads. However, the journey is better than it used to be and the tarmac is gradually being extended towards the Mara.

The first sight of this natural wonderland with its abundance of

A view of the Masai Mara National Reserve from the Mara Serena Lodge, with its rondavel rooms blending in with the African scenery.

game species, makes it all worthwhile. Here the great herds of immense shuffling elephants browse among the rich, tree-studded grasslands with an occasional sighting of the solitary rhino. Thomson's gazelles, zebra and eland and many more species of plains game offer a rich choice of food for the predatory lions, leopards and cheetahs which hunt within the Masai Mara's wilderness.

The Mara river every now and then comes into tumultuous flood; I have been trapped within the game park by the rising waters and had to take a plane out, leaving the car to be collected two weeks later. In the river you will see hippos submerge at the approach of a tourist bus before breaking surface to snort and submerge again. They are really plentiful and up to 50 can be seen in the pools if you are fortunate. Drowsy-looking crocodile sunbathe on the river banks, mouths agape but ever watchful for their next meal. But all of this is secondary to the march of the wildebeest. Each year, far south in the great Serengeti, they will raise their heads, sniff the air and, as if answering a military command, turn in unison and start the long trek to the Kenya border and beyond.

The spectacle of so many of these creatures moving as a great mass across the savannah, in a lemming-like fashion, is one of the most astonishing sights in nature. The herds are following the rains, and when they arrive in the Mara there is new succulent grass to eat. But the trek is costly. Blindly heading north, accompanied by packs of predators – hyenas, the big cats and the circling ever-watchful vultures – hundreds, perhaps thousands, of the lame, laggard and sick will never reach their destination. Still more die in the swirling flood waters while trying to across the Mara river.

Once the rains have ended and the grass begins to wither under the harsh sun, the wildebeest once again turn south, heading hundreds of miles back into the Seregneti.

The actual migration does not last for very many days and its start is impossible to foretell accurately. Nevertheless, visitors to the Masai Mara in August through September are certain to see the great herds of wildebeest and zebra together with their attendant predators.

All year round the Mara is rich in resident wildlife – there are always plenty of lion; a nursery group (lionesses and cubs) of 21 is the most I have seen together at one place. Apart from the better-known species already mentioned there are many opportunities to add some of the rare and less-frequently-seen animals to the visitor's checklist, such as the roan antelope and bat-eared fox. There are also thousands of topi, not found elsewhere except in the Tsavo Park. You may also come across the fascinating sight of a pack of wild dogs hunting out.

The combination of gentle climate, scenic splendour and unbelievable wildlife makes the Masai Mara Kenya's most popular inland destination.

There is a good choice of nearby accommodation: at Keekorok Lodge, Mara Serena Lodge, Governor's Camp and Little Governor's Camp.

Meru

Meru is the great national reserve which became world famous as the place in which Joy Adamson's lioness Elsa was returned to the wild. It lies less than 320 km (200 miles) from Nairobi via the new highly scenic road linking Embu to Meru, completed at the end of 1983.

Of all the parks Meru presents the widest variety of landscapes and habitats. Forest, swamp and savannah are pierced by 15 perennial rivers rising on the Mount Kenya massif and all destined to reach the River Tana which, just south of the equator, forms the park's lower boundary. In this marvellous wilderness a great variety of wildlife exists, some in huge quantities; as well as the Big Five there is a herd of the white rhino re-established in the 1970s after centuries of declining numbers. Incidentally, don't expect the rhino to be white as the word is a corruption of the Afrikaans 'wit', meaning wide; the white rhino has a wider mouth than the common rhino. The park is

Meru Mulika Lodge in the Meru game park, designed traditionally.

also one of the best in which to see both leopard and cheetah, although the former has so far eluded me.

Meru's closeness to Mount Kenya and the Nyambene Hills, which reach 2515 m (8250 ft), ensures a good rainfall and the park is therefore lush and green for most of the year. The park is also alive with birds – game birds are especially prolific.

Accommodation is at Meru Mulika Lodge and Leopard Rock.

Mount Elgon and Saiwa Swamp

Mount Elgon, whose peaks reach 4321 m (14,178 ft), lies astride the Kenya-Uganda border. Named after the El Kony, a small break-away group of Masai, its immense bulk, like most of the other great mountains of East Africa, is the remains of a former volcano. Most of such volcanoes are associated with the intense subterranean activity which brought about the Great Rift Valley.

There is no permanent snow on the mountain but the bleak peaks are surrounded with the typical afro-alpine vegetation of the high mountains of the equator. Giant groundsel and giant lobelia grow over the 3500 m (12,000 ft) level and for much of the year everlasting flowers cover moorlands as far as the eye can see. At lower levels giant heath, bamboo and montane forest prevail, and in these areas there are elephant and plenty of buffalo. Part of the east flank is set aside as the Mount Elgon National Park, stretching from the peaks to the boundary of the forest and the heavily cultivated country of the Luhya people. Within the park is a multitude of wildlife and flowers and some exciting oddities – among them the Elgon caves, two of which in particular, Kitum and Makingeny, have been largely gouged out over thousands of years by the small forest elephants, apparently to get at the sodium sulphate in the walls.

Mount Elgon has been called Kenya's loneliest park, but that is unfair. It is an eye-feasting spectacle for the visitor with scenic beauty in mind and unusual experience for the inquisitive traveller.

Saiwa Swamp National Park

Not far from Mount Elgon and only 24 km (15 miles) from Kitale is the tiny 191 hectare (473 acre) Saiwa Swamp National Park. Created primarily for the protection of the rare Sitatunga antelope, the park is a perfect example of how a very small area can survive as a complete ecological unit. The Sitatunga, which relies on a swamp habitat, has evolved to survive in such conditions, and despite the minute size of the park will continue to do so. The Sitatunga are numerous enough for there to be almost a guaranteed chance of seeing them.

Accommodation can be found at Mount Elgon Lodge and the Sirikwa Hotel, and at the Eldoret for Saiwa.

Nairobi National Park

Nairobi National Park which lies just 10 km (about 6 miles) from the heart of the capital, was established in 1946. It comprises mostly savannah, with a large stock of migratory game, and lies between the Nairobi-Mombasa railway and the suburb of Langata. It is open on its south-east perimeter and here the Kitengela Conservation Area allows a corridor for the natural migration of the game, which takes place with the seasonal rains.

Well laid out, with exceptionally-well-maintained roads, the park is a model for all others, both physically and administratively. Speed limits are rigidly imposed and the park closes at 6.30 p.m.

Of the most popular species, only the elephant is an absentee, but the rest – leopard, lion, buffalo and rhino – as well as a multitude of other creatures, are well represented here, although the leopard is as elusive as ever.

The Athi river at the park's far end forms a delightful natural demarcation, and provides walks through a forest heavily populated with many species of monkey and a wide variety of birds and, in the river pools, hippo and an occasional crocodile.

Large populations of giraffe, wildebeest, eland and Thomson's gazelle dominate the plains of the park, with strutting secretary birds and powerful ostrich as attractive counterpoints. The park's prides of lion are well-observed by park staff and an inquiry at the gate when entering will usually reveal their approximate whereabouts. Cheetah, too, have made the park famous.

Even if the felines are being shy there is more than enough within this suburban wilderness to delight the wildlife lovers and the casual tourist. In addition to the Athi river, the Mbagathi gorge provides a dramatic boundary on the southern side and leopard certainly have their lairs there.

The park's animal orphanage, at the main gate, offers an extra spectacle before or after visiting the park. Here waifs, strays and the lame are brought for rest and recuperation. Although not a zoo, the

orphanage does house animals not indigenous to Kenya – sometimes gifts to Kenya or perhaps leftovers from visiting circuses. The orphanage has a well maintained veterinary hospital. Here, eagles and carnivores have been treated for near fatal wounds and the hospital staff acted as foster parents to one orphan baby elephant.

But the spectacle is in the park itself, where it is often possible to see lions sunning themselves by the side of the road, or cheetah languidly inspecting the plains for a kill.

Samburu, Buffalo Springs and Shaba

Samburu National Reserve lies 330 km (205 miles) from Nairobi in

the hot and arid fringes of the vast northern region of Kenya. It contains a number of wildlife species rarely found elsewhere in any numbers, including Grevy's zebra and the shy long-necked gerenuk, a remarkable antelope which spends much of its time on its two hind legs searching for succulent leaves among the withered scrub trees which dot this sparse terrain.

Dramatic Samburu swelters under the harsh equatorial sun for most of the year, but relief comes from the wide swathe of the Ewaso Ngiro river, which rises hundreds of miles to the west in the Aberdares and vanishes beyond Samburu in the Lorian Swamp.

The river is at its best in the reserve, broad and often sluggish, with a large population of crocodile and hippo, seen frequently at almost every meandering bend – the crocodile basking in the sun and the hippo breaking surface at regular intervals to suck in air noisily.

Elephant roam the gaunt hills which punctuate the scrubland and where occasional clusters of the vividly-coloured desert rose break the monotonous aridity. These elephant seek solace in the shallow waters of the river and from time to time visitors find herds drinking and bathing in obvious contentment.

Along the Ewaso Ngiro's banks clusters of doum palm and riverside forest add shade and contrast to the surrounding country-side and provide a habitat for many varieties of primate.

Buffalo Springs

The reserve is immediately adjacent to the smaller but equally attractive Buffalo Springs National reserve, established some time later. With a similar environment, Buffalo Springs takes its name from an oasis of crystal clear water, and plays host to similar species of game and aquatic life.

These two reserves, with the Shaba National Reserve, which lies to the east on the opposite side of the Great North Road from Isiolo to Moyale, form a trio of unusual and attractive game sanctuaries very different from others in Kenya.

Shaba

Shaba has a particular place in the history of Kenyan game conservation for it was in this reserve that the authoress Joy Adamson was murdered in early 1980, her trilogy of books on the rehabilitation of leopard to the wild unfinished. The reserve takes its name from a cone of volcanic rock and evidence of the intensity of its upheavals is demonstrated by the huge lava flow that the traveller has to cross to reach this remote wilderness.

The reserve's northern border is marked by the wide, sauntering flow of the Ewaso Ngiro on its way to the Lorian Swamp – the tall trees of the stark riverside forest in sharp contrast to the rugged and pitted tracts which make up much of the sanctuary. Many small hills break up the landscape in Shaba and, with four springs, the reserve is better watered than its neighbours.

Shaba is a place for the connoisseur where the quality of the experience exceeds the quality of the wildlife.

Accommodation for the three reserves is available at Samburu

Lodge, Buffalo Springs Tented Camp, River Lodge and Shaba Tented Camp. (Tented camps are hotels where the rooms are individual tents).

Shimba Hills, Taita Hills and Lakes Jipe and Chala

The Shimba Hills is a forested plateau rising 450 m (1500 ft) out of the coastal plain, an enchanting world, lonely and remote from the heat and bustle below.

Although not significantly higher than the equatorial heat of Kenya's coastal strip, the Shimba Hills are remarkably cool; the Indian Ocean monsoons rise over the eastward escarpment with invigorating freshness.

This land of rolling grasslands and forests of giant, primeval trees is home to a remarkable variety of wildlife – including 400 elephant who favour the vine-like fruit of the borassus palm. Lion and leopard lurk in the forest areas, often heard but not seen. But most distinctive of the many species in the park's 1922 square kilometres (742) square miles) area is the rare Sable antelope found in the same habitat as the several large herds of buffalo.

Picnic sites on either side of the escarpment provide superb views – to the east overlooking the distant turquoise of the Indian Ocean, and to the west hazy views of the vast plains, the Taita Hills rising up out of them like a misty giant and beyond, on days of exceptional clarity, the mighty mass of Kilimanjaro.

Unspoilt, one of the least exploited of all Kenya's game reserves, the combination of rolling grassland and forest, hill and dale, and shadowy animals make these hills a true delight for all nature lovers. A landing strip on one of the highest points provides a destination for long-distance travellers but the park is a short drive from Mombasa or any other of the south coast hotels. There is no accommodation in the Shimba Hills.

Taita Hills

The Taita Hills Game Sanctuary is a 11,300 hectare (28,000 acre) private ranch on which are sited the Taita Hills Lodge and Salt Lick Lodge. The sanctuary contains elephant, lion, cheetah, buffalo and a host of other wildlife which, at certain times of the year, can be plentiful. Much of the game visits a water hole over which Salt Lick Lodge is built.

Lake Jipe

The Taita Hills is a useful base for a visit to Lake Jipe, which has protection as part of Tsavo West National Park. The lake, bisected by the border with Tanzania, is a favourite haunt of bird watchers, and the national park authorities provide boats for hire to serious ornithologists.

Lake Chala

Another lake shared by both Tanzania and Kenya is Lake Chala, now easily reached from a new road linking Taveta with Loitokitok. Its deep, midnight blue waters attract a host of legends about serpents and monsters, yet to be substantiated.

Accommodation is available at Taita Hills Lodge and Salt Lick Lodge.

Tana River Primate National Reserve

Although the reserve is small, only 168 square kilometres (65 square miles), it contains certain elements quite unique to any wildlife sanctuary in Kenya. As the name suggests, it was established to protect a small number of primates which have no other location in the country. There are two species involved, the Red Colobus and the Crested Mangabey. These also occur in the tropical rain forests of western Uganda and Zaire and are indicative of the time, centuries ago, when these great forests covered the whole of Africa – west to east. The reserve is a mixture of savannah and riverside forest, often of exquisite beauty. Both the common and reticulated giraffe and both species of zebra are found, as well as the oryx, buffalo and lesser kudu. But the real adventure is a boat ride on the swirling brown waters of the Tana River, which abounds with hippo and crocodile – and of course a galaxy of water birds.

You can get accommodation at Baomo Lodge, 160 km (100 miles) from Malindi.

Tsavo National Park

The combined area of Tsavo East and West National Parks makes Tsavo one of the largest game sanctuaries in the world – larger in size than Wales. It covers more than 20,000 square kilometres (7720 square miles) and lies roughly half-way between Mombasa and Nairobi.

Tsavo West

The first lodge inside any national park was opened at Kilaguni by the Duke of Gloucester in 1962. It stands almost at the centre of Tsavo West and offers excellent game runs in any direction. It has an almost permanent and semi-tame squirrel, hyrax and mongoose population, numerous species of bird and an almost ever present herd of elephant. This, however, is only a fraction of the natural delights which Tsavo West has to offer – there are more than 60 mammal species commonly to be found in the park, 400 bird species and over 1000 plant species.

Poachers and drought caused great devastation among the park's elephant and rhino populations in the past, but both are recovering. There are somewhere between 6000 and 8000 elephant and roughly 100 rhino. A model national park in both layout and its geographical, animal and plant diversity, Tsavo West has more than 2000 km (1250 miles) of well-maintained marram roads, well signposted to lead from one natural wonder to another.

Chief among these is Mzima Springs, replenishing the 20 million litres (4 million gallons) of crystal-clear water a day from the underground reservoirs of the nearby Chyulu Hills. The springs form a haven for a rich variety of wildlife including wallowing elephants, light-footed but ponderous-looking hippo, apparently weightless in the water as they tiptoe across the bottom, crocodiles basking on the bank or swirling through the waters, together with the usual hoofed animals, chattering birds and monkeys. The water from these springs has for many years provided the main supply for Mombasa. An observation platform, well marked trails and an underwater viewing window provide varied vantage points to enjoy this remarkable oasis.

Not far from Mzima Springs, along a well marked track, lies the precipitous magnificence of the Ngulia escarpment at the foot of the Ngulia Hills, which rise to 1821 m (5974 ft). Each year, during the autumn season of the northern hemisphere, Ngulia has become the base of a unique phenomenon. Attracted by the lights of Ngulia Lodge Hotel thousands of migrant birds descend through the mists, prevalent at this time of year, to find themselves being netted and ringed. It provides vital information on the migratory routes and habits of many species of bird common in the northern hemisphere. More than 60,000 birds of 40 species have been ringed to date.

The prolific wildlife includes many lion – some undoubtedly descendants of the infamous man-eaters of Tsavo written about in J. H. Patterson's book. Among the less common animals to be found are the fringe-eared oryx, the gerenuk and Hunter's hartebeest. Other carnivores to be seen are leopard, cheetah, wild dog, caracal and hyena.

The landscape is dominated, especially off the hills, by the giant baobab trees which live as long as 1000 years. After the rains the park is covered in a riot of blossoms, the acacia trees showered white and pink and the desert rose, like a miniature baobab, produces flowers of striking beauty.

The feast of wildlife, flora and birds combines to make Tsavo of special interest – an interest made greater perhaps by the geological activity shown by massive lava flows from recently extinct volcanoes, as at Shaba.

Tsavo East

Only a small area of this vast nature reserve, larger by far than Tsavo West, is open to the public. The remainder provides a remote animal wilderness. However, there are many interesting aspects in the open area of Tsavo East, not least the spine of the Yatta Plateau, one of the world's longest petrified lava flows, and the rushing waters of the Athi River.

Downstream the Athi forms Lugard Falls, a long stretch of rippling water cataracts which is a favourite haunt of sunbathing crocodiles, before it meanders on, now as the Galana, down to the sea.

The falls gush through a small fissure, narrow enough for some to risk standing astride, before the river drops to Crocodile Point below. The falls were named after Britain's first proconsul in Africa, Frederick Lugard.

Unlike the western half, Tsavo East is subject to ferocious droughts, and Aruba Dam – built in 1952 – even dried up completely in 1961, although it covers an area of 85 hectares (211 acres). Although this wilderness is hostile to man it is nevertheless inhabited by a very wide range of plains game – zebra, antelope and ostrich, as well as the great elephant herds which plunder their way through bush and forest to the permanent waters of the Athi.

There is accommodation in the parks themselves. In Tsavo West it is at Kilaguni Lodge and Ngulia Lodge, and in Tsavo East at Voi Safari Lodge and Tsavo Safari Tented Camp. Near the parks you can stay at Tsavo Inn, Crocodile Camp, Taita Hills Lodge and Salt Lick Lodge.

7 Nairobi

Nairobi got its name from a stream named Usao Nairobi – cold water, in the Masai language. The rains apart, it has one of the best climates in the world. It's never too hot, but the sun shines, and it's never too humid or too cold. However, there was no logical reason for the town to be sited there except that it seemed like a good place to have a station and watering point for the trains during the construction of the Uganda railway. When mile 327 was reached on 30 May 1899, it was at a place known by the Masai as 'The beginning of all beauty'. Ronald Preston, the line's railhead engineer, disagreed remarking that it was 'a bleak swampy stretch of soppy landscape, devoid of human habitation of any sort, the resort of thousands of wild animals of every species'. He added that it 'did not boast one single tree' – not a hopeful beginning for a town that has shaped the future of East Africa!

It was an important spot for the railway, though; after leaving mile 327 the tracks had to climb nearly 600 m (2000 ft) over a distance of just 43 km (27 miles). It was an intricate and punishing task which could not be controlled from the coast, so a staging post had to be constructed. Since this was the last piece of level ground before reaching the Rift Valley, it was the obvious choice.

What started off as a railhead, accommodating the staff and equipment for this huge undertaking, was founded as a town in 1901 and has now become one of the great towns of Africa. Within months of being established there were turntables, marshalling yards, workshops, stores and houses; not long after came the water supply, then there was a regular Mombasa to Nairobi train service.

Sir Charles Eliot, who moved the Protectorate's headquarters from Mombasa to Nairobi in 1902, remarked that 'the beauty of a view in Nairobi depends upon the more or less thorough elimination of the town from the landscape'. Fortunately things have changed, and

The rising skyline of Nairobi, with the international Kenyatta Conference Centre in the middle of the picture and the Uhuru Park in the foreground.

there are no longer any swamps; trees are everywhere and the marshalling yards and railway no longer dominate the life and landscape of the town.

The humble town now boasts a population approaching one million, a number the local populace seems to be busy trying to increase. It's also about as cosmopolitan as you are likely to get outside South Africa; there are tall skyscrapers, conference centres,

casinos, ethnic restaurants, discos and the rest. A new sports centre is
being built with money from China. Everyone is keen to give aid to
Kenya which still remains one of the most democratic countries on
the African continent.

It is the commercial and business capital of the country, as well as
the main port of entry into Kenya and therefore the tourist centre of
the country. From Nairobi you can go up to the Rift Valley, Nakuru
and Naivasha, to Lake Bogoria and Lake Baringo, and to Mount
Kenya, or you can take the bus to Lake Turkana – a dusty eight-day
adventure to a magical part of the country. West will take you to the
great Masai Mara game reserve which lies on the border with
Tanzania. South West takes you to Amboseli Game Park, lying under
the shadow of the magnificent Mount Kilimanjaro.

However, Nairobi is much more than the gateway to the rest of the
country, it is a fascinating place in its own right. As with any
developing country there are beggars and sights that the first-timer
will find unpleasant, but don't let that overcome the positive aspects
of the country. Nairobi is a treasure trove for the shopper, but
requiring some persistence and perspicacity; in other words, don't
believe everything you are told. For instance, there are numerous
street hawkers selling what they say are elephant hair bracelets; if it
really were there would be an awful lot of bald elephants in Kenya!

Shopping

Although there are one or two familiar names, such as Woolworth,
most of the shops in central Nairobi are individually owned, run on
the old-fashioned system of having someone behind a counter to
serve. The main shopping area is confined to an area bordered by
Koinange Street on the west side, Mama Ngina Street on the south,
Biashara Street at the north and Tom Mboya Street to the east.
Within this area are the main shopping streets of Kenyatta Avenue,
Kimathi Street and Muindi Mbingu Street, intersected by a dozen
other smaller streets all with packed shops and hopeful proprietors.

The main items on sale, and the ones the tourist is most likely to
want, are the local artifacts and curios. They will be available from
street stalls, the market and shops, so have a good look round before
buying. The type of souvenirs available include heads, statues,
animals and groups, mostly carved from wood. You will notice that
some carvings have a black centre and a piece of white bark on the
exterior; this is to prove it is made from ebony, which is why it will be

so expensive. If the price sounds too cheap it isn't ebony.

Other souvenirs available are soapstone carvings such as chess sets, snake boxes, hippo boxes, soap dishes and animals. Jewellery is also big business here and you will be amazed by the ingenuity of the artists, who seem to be able to make something pretty out of the most unlikely metal items such as zips and nails. The bracelets are always a good buy, as the style is continually changing. If you go to the markets a number of times over a long period you will see the evolution of particular designs. There are other jewellery items made from beads which are also quite beautiful and irresistible.

A good place to start looking is the Market (the main entrance is in Muindi Mbingu Street) where there will be examples of almost everything on show, from carved masks to spears. It is also a major fruit, vegetable and flower market, so be prepared to face the gauntlet of the grocery sellers before finding the artifacts. One of the really popular items in the market are baskets, of which there are numerous traders – mostly out the back – and deals for large quantities are easily made. On sale also are rather poor quality batiks and banana leaf paintings. These are rather uninteresting and probably unlikely to last the trip home in the suitcase, so I wouldn't recommend them.

If the market looks to be housed in a curious shaped building – rather like a small hangar – it is because it was originally built in the 1930s to house airships; following the R101 airship disaster the plan was scrapped but the building was retained.

To see the top quality gifts it is a good idea to go to the African Heritage shop in Kenyatta Avenue – probably straight after you have been to the market. Here they not only have the best of Kenyan gifts, old and new, but also many from other parts of the continent. Here is one of the few places where you can find genuine tribal crafts.

For cloth of all types, from silk to prints, you can't do much better than Biashara Street. Bookshops also abound in Nairobi, so take advantage of them and buy a good reference work on animals, and one on birds as well. If you can't find what you need try the Select Bookshop (the largest in town they claim) which is in the Mutual Building, Kimathi Street. For safari-type clothes you can try your hotel shop or shops in Kimathi Street, and Wabera Street, but also look around; many have similar clothes and the prices will vary.

Gems and silverware can be found everywhere but it is also too easy to be fooled, so go to a reputable shop. Although there are some precious jewels available most shops specialise in semi-precious stones, look out for rubies and the usual opals, amethysts, jade and aquamarines and the more unusual and local tsavorite (a type of green garnet) and tanzanite (a blue sapphire-like stone). Also available is the intriguing amber, but beware: if you can see into it or find a seam then it is plastic. Instead of buying a string why not buy individual matching pieces and string them yourself.

For those who are very interested in geology and gemstones there is a museum open to the public at the Mines and Geological Department, Madini House, Machakos Road. You could also try the main Nairobi Museum.

Places to See

Nairobi Museum

No visit to Nairobi would be complete without looking in at the museum on Museum Hill. It is only 2 km (just over a mile) from the centre of town, but take a taxi (check the price first) arranged from the hotel. It is well set out, though in places a little more thought could have gone into some of the exhibits, particularly that of the animals which is, at present, a crescent of stuffed bodies on wooden plinths. However, there are good displays of tribal crafts and flora – including a fascinating set of watercolours by Joy Adamson. There is also a display of her paintings of tribesmen and women. There is a small display devoted to the Mau Mau, the freedom fighters of the 1950s, and of the Leakey discoveries. There are multilingual tours available. Opening times are 9.30 a.m. to 6 p.m. daily, including holidays.

The Snake Park

In the grounds of the Museum is the Snake Park, which is also well worth a visit. There are around fifty species of snake and reptile, including alligators and crocodiles. Someone obviously had fun writing the signs; there is 'Trespassers will be eaten' over the crocodile enclosure and 'Do not litter, or you will be requested to retrieve it' over the snake pit. Next to the snake pit is a small aquarium, and an aviary with indigenous African birds. Opening times are as for the Museum.

The Railway Museum

With the railway playing such an important part in the history of the

Beady-eyed and dangerous it might be, but this nilotic crocodile can be seen quite safely at the Nairobi Snake Park.

country, you should try a visit to the Railway Museum, located near the railway station off Haile Selassie Avenue. You don't need to be a steam buff to appreciate it, just interested in history, although for the enthusiasts it must seem like heaven. It is even possible to come away with a small momento of the old East African Railway in the shape of brass plates. The museum contains the history of the line and has some excellent photographs of the construction, as well as the coach in which the unfortunate Charles Ryall, a Superintendent of Police, was killed by a lion in 1900.

Other Nairobi attractions include the City Park (4 km/2·5 miles from the city centre) which has a fine collection of rare plants as well as a maze. This is located on the Limuru Road. Along State House Road is the Arboretum but don't go there alone at night.

You may also visit the Parliament Buildings, which are located at the intersection of Uhuru Highway and Harambee Avenue. Uhuru, by the way, means freedom, and, as mentioned, Harambee is the national slogan.

Off the Langata Road is the Bomas of Kenya – a cultural centre where it is possible to see local tribes dancing twice a day, usually early afternoon and mid-evening; at weekends the afternoon show is a little later. There are also genuine-looking African huts and villages which can be inspected, while your hunger and thirst can be quenched at a reasonably-priced restaurant.

Several parks offer walks among a mixture of exotic and indigenous flowers, shrubs and trees. In October more than a quarter of a million jacaranda trees burst into an electric blue to add a new richness of colour to this already colourful land.

For the more exercise minded there is the new sports complex with an athletics track, ten golf courses, including the Royal Nairobi Golf Club, and a number of cricket, rugby and football grounds, tennis, badminton and squash courts. And, of course, there are swimming pools at every hotel.

Horse racing and polo are other favourites of the town and the former can be seen at the Nairobi racecourse, which meets regularly throughout the year. The Limuru Country Club also boasts a racecourse, as well as a golf course but at 27 km (17 miles) from Nairobi it is a little far out for a day trip. If polo is your game then the club which meets at Jamhuri Park on Wednesdays, Saturdays and Sundays welcomes visitors.

If you are more interested in motorsport there is a race track on the road to Jomo Kenyatta International Airport, and the famous annual Safari Rally, which virtually brings the country to a standstill every Easter, such is the interest. It is a quite spectaclar event, and worth a detour to take in one of the special stages – if you are lucky enough to be in the country at the right time.

Night Life

The night life is varied and ranges from the saucy to the sophisticated; it is quite easy to acquire company within a few seconds of entering some establishments. There are night clubs with authentic

African music, while others offer shows of the international type, although not always with internationally known people – but certainly at international prices!

There are 15 cinemas, including two drive-ins, which show the latest films – see the newspapers for the details. There is also the Phoenix Players with a resident group of professional actors who perform a wide variety of works, mostly modern, and all in English. The French Cultural Centre organises special film shows, concerts and talks, and the World Wildlife Fund has regular wildlife films- – details of which can be obtained from your hotel.

Worship

If you wish to go to church on a Sunday there are a few to choose from, and you should ask your hotel desk clerk for the nearest for your particular denomination.

Restaurants and Eating Out

There is a wide selection of restaurants in Nairobi, with cuisine ranging from African and Indian to excellent French and Italian. If you require a detailed list there are specialist restaurant guidebooks; in this section I will offer a few alternatives to your hotel.

African
The best of the African restaurants is the **African Heritage** on Banda Street where the prices are as reasonable as the food. On Saturdays you have the added pleasure of live music which is also usually good. At lunchtime the menu is devoted to African cuisine while in the evenings it specialises in Ethiopian food, either indoors or on the terrace. The **New Stanley Hotel** offers a taste of Africa every Wednesday lunchtime.

Seafood
Seafood is the speciality of **Alan Bobbe's Bistro** at Caltex House on Koinange Street, although it does do other dishes as well. It is also one of the best restaurants in town, with Mr Bobbe taking a keen interest in everything that happens. It is essential to book, and expect a relatively expensive meal in the evenings. The **Tamarind** restaurant at National Bank House, Harambee Avenue, is a seafood speciality restaurant and, although, expensive the food is excellent.

Many religions are practised in Kenya, with the Muslims having some of the most spectacular buildings. This one is the Jamia mosque.

Western

Western food is readily available, and very good it is too. The best restaurant is probably **The Horseman** at Karen, a suburb of Nairobi named after Karen Blixen – what a nice way to be remembered! It has a mixture of French and Italian cooking which leans towards nouvelle cuisine, although the quantites are quite adequate. I have never had a bad meal there and the service has always been excellent and attentive.

One of the favourites with westerners is **The Carnivore** which, as you would expect from the name, is a meat eaters' paradise, with almost every kind of meat imaginable being cooked over a charcoal pit. It is an open air Brazilian style restaurant arranged round this pit. There are menus for children and even vegetarians; it is quite expensive – but worth a visit.

The French Cultural Centre houses **Le Jardin De Paris** on Monrovia and Lolita Street which, as you would expect, has a bistro atmosphere with music and excellent wines. It is good and not too expensive.

For something not quite as expensive and exclusive try the **El Patio** restaurant on the mezzanine floor of the Reinsurance Plaza Building by Nkrumah Lane. It has a wide menu and very helpful staff.

Also reasonably priced is the **Pizzeria** at the Hilton Hotel, which not only serves a good imitation of a pizza but also a range of Italian dishes.

But for a better style of Italian food there is the **Trattoria** on the junction of Wabera and Kaunda Streets. Not only is the food genuine but it has excellent ice creams as well.

Eastern

Eastern restaurants are fairly easy to come by with the country having a sizeable Asian minority. For an up-market curry there is the **Safeer** restaurant in the Hotel Ambassadeur, Tom Mboya Street, and the two **Minar** restaurants, one on Banda Street and the other in the Sarit Centre, Westlands. You could also try the Supreme Hotel's **Mayur** restaurant, which is not only exclusively vegetarian but also air conditioned – what a combination!

If your tastes are more for the Chinese style of cooking then the **Hong Kong** restaurant on Koinange Street is a good bet, although the décor is somewhat lacklustre. A moderately priced and popular Chinese restaurant is the **Mandarin** on Tom Mboya Street, and there is also the **Tin Tin** in the Kenyatta Conference Centre.

One other that you may find interesting is the **Japanese** restaurant in Standard Street in the shadow of the Six-Eighty Hotel. The menu is easy to understand and the staff extremely helpful.

If you require a snack or cup of coffee and if you are not already staying at the Inter-Continental, Serena, New Stanley or Norfolk Hotels then any of these are ideal. The Thorn Tree (the coffee shop at the New Stanley Hotel) is particularly famous as a pavement restaurant and meeting place; if you wait long enough the whole of Nairobi will pass you by, and it is famous as a place where messages can be left and received.

The Norfolk Hotel's terrace restaurant is *the* place to take a cup of coffee or beer or even a light snack.

The Serena and Intercontinental pools are the best from almost every angle, providing good swimming, company and snacks.

Hotels

All hotels listed here are first class and are those generally used by most tour companies. All will have private bathrooms with each room. It is not a complete list by any means as there are around twenty-two hotels of varying quality in Nairobi.

The newest and most exclusive hotel is the **Mount Kenya Safari Club** hotel on University Way. Membership is required before you can book a room. Naturally, this can be done at the same time, and it will allow also you to visit the up-country Mount Kenya Safari Club.

The **Nairobi Serena** hotel in Central Park is an excellent hotel with the sort of facilities the more discerning traveller has come to expect. The rooms are fairly spacious with large windows – all the better to see out across the park and towards the jagged skyline of Nairobi, less than a kilometre away. They are all equipped with air conditioning, bath and shower, a radio and phone. Other amenities include the restaurant, coffee shop and grill room as well as the barbeque terrace and cocktail lounge. There is a swimming pool where food can be ordered, plus hotel shops. Squash, tennis and golf can be played nearby while table tennis is provided at the pool.

The **Norfolk Hotel**, on Harry Thuku Road, is not only Nairobi's oldest and most famous hotel, it is the best known hotel in the country after Tree Tops. It was first opened on Christmas Day 1904, but has undergone several changes to make it a five-star international standard hotel. It has satisfied stars, millionaires and writers (including Ernest Hemingway) as well as royalty, and so has become part of the history of the country. You can still hear stories of safaris here if you stand at the bar on the terrace. Standard of service is high as the personal touch is still valued. For accommodation you have the choice of the newer hotel rooms or the older traditional rooms, but whichever you choose they all have their own private bath and phone. There is a dining room, grill room, cocktail lounge and the terrace. In the courtyard be sure not to miss the aviaries housing a number of exotic African birds, as well as the not so exotic which have been enticed in there by the abundant food. There is also a pool which is fairly secluded and parts are in shade for some of the day.

The **Intercontinental** hotel is a popular staging post for the airlines as it is conveniently situated near the centre of Nairobi and on the direct route to the airport. It is very much an international hotel with the usual phones and radios in the rooms, with television on request, as well as a balcony for each one and air conditioning. There are several eating points on the ground floor and on the rooftop, where they have speciality lunches and evening meals and where there is a cocktail lounge which also has dancing. During the day you can take advantage of the terrace restaurant by the swimming pool. There are also the usual tourist shops, a hairdresser and a bank.

The **Hilton International,** Nairobi, is very centrally placed on Moi Avenue and Mama Ngina Street, and is also difficult to miss, being a 20-storey round edifice jutting into the skyline. It is well appointed with phone, radio and colour television in each room, as well as air conditioning. There is ample eating, with a restaurant, pizzeria, grill room, cocktail bar and lounge, and a late night coffee shop. The swimming pool is several storeys up but has its own snack facilities. There is also a health club and a number of shops in the building.

The **New Stanley** hotel on the corner of Kenyatta Avenue and Kimathi Street is extremely central for the main shopping areas of the town. There has been a hotel on the site since 1907, although the present incumbent is fairly modern, with most rooms having air conditioning. All do have radio and phone and some have balconies. Apart from the ever-popular Thorn Tree Restaurant on the pavement there is a restaurant and bar and some shops. Although it is a luxury class hotel it is not in the first division.

The **Six-Eighty** hotel is another centrally located hotel, very popular with conferences. It has a whole floor given over to restaurants and bars, both indoor and outdoor. Rooms are of a high standard with radio and phone, although there is no television available. No swimming pool but the usual shopping arcade and beauty parlour.

Car Hire

Most companies will not only have ordinary cars, but campers, station wagons and four-wheel-drive vehicles as well. To hire a car you must be over 23 years old, and a deposit will be required unless you have either a Visa card, American Express or Diners Club.

8 Mombasa and the Tropical Coastline

Mombasa is Kenya's second largest town and the oldest – with a history which stretches back almost 2000 years. The first recorded evidence of its existence was reported by Diogenes, the Greek traveller, in the second century. The town is built on an island midway along the Kenya coast, south of the equator. Less than a century ago it was connected to the mainland for the first time by what was then the Uganda Railway.

To the north a new toll bridge (the New Nyali Bridge) spans Tudor Creek, with views of the old harbour, linking the town with beach resorts that stretch along the north coast.

On the south side a frequent car and passenger ferry service plies across Kilindi Creek, close to the entrance to the modern port area, and carrying tourists to the splendid beach resorts on the south coast.

Mombasa town itself is a mystical, hot and sticky mixture of ancient and modern, with a cosmopolitan population blending Europe, Africa, Arabia and Asia. The people who live in this old but vibrant gateway to Kenya and Africa now number nearly 400,000.

Fringing the old harbour, still used by dhows, is the old town, a maze of narrow streets and pedestrian lanes, lined with quaint shuttered houses and open-fronted shops. The smell of spices is always present. Dominating the entrance to the dhow harbour and overlooking the old town is Fort Jesus, built by the Portuguese in the last decade of the sixteenth century. The fort is open to visitors and contains a museum displaying antiquities, both civilian and military, from the length of the Kenya coast.

A wide choice of African curios, together with some antiques – and some that look older than they are – are available from shops and pavement vendors, but a shopping highlight is a visit to Biashara Street where shops compete for the purchaser's eye and pocket with dazzling displays of locally-woven fabrics and prints. You should also

A tropical coastline indeed, with mile upon mile of golden, sandy beaches fronting the warm waters of the Indian Ocean.

take an excursion into the municipal market on Digo Road where you are able to try all sorts of strange and exotic vegetables and spices. Continue on down the Digo Road to the roundabout and turn right into Moi Avenue; a short way along you will see the giant symbol of Mombasa, four huge elephant tusks spanning the dual carriageway. The Moi Avenue and Digo Road intersection point is a major shopping area for Arabic goods, as well as gemstones, herbs and fabrics. Near the elephant tusks is the Information Bureau of

Mombasa and the Coast Tourist Association, where the helpful staff will provide maps, advice and information.

Worth seeing also are the Hindu temples, with their superb decorated entrances and interiors. One even has a white spire topped with solid gold.

From Mombasa it is possible to make short excursions to many of the beach resorts, or alternatively to Mtwapa Creek with its ocean-arium, dhow trips and water skiing. Deep sea game fishing is easily arranged from Mombasa itself – either through the Outrigger Hotel or the Bahari Club, which is on the north mainland facing the old harbour.

If you require a drop of refreshment on your tour round the town then just below Fort Jesus, still on the Nkrumah Road, is the Mombasa Club which, for a few shillings temporary membership, will provide a relaxing haven from the bustle and heat of the town. Across town there is the Outrigger Hotel or the Mombasa Yacht Club, which once again offers reasonably priced temporary member-ship and the use of its pool.

The coastal strip is now fairly densely populated and the animals which have survived have done so by virtue of their ability to remain hidden; you are unlikely to see any large ones unless you drive through a patch of forest at night, visit the Shimba Hill Game Reserve or venture beyond the Tana River.

Occasionally the lions get hungry and cross the causeway onto Mombasa Island – in 1945 three crossed over and proceeded to maul several of the inhabitants before being driven away.

Monkeys, including yellow baboons, are common, and vervet monkeys are often attracted to human habitations, particularly hotels. Bushbabies and their larger relatives, the greater galagos, are common, though nocturnal. The greater galago is very partial to palm wine and will often steal it before the tapper is able to remove it from the tree, a failing which proves their undoing as they are very easy to catch once drunk!

Snakes are not as common at the coast as one might expect and since they are shy you rarely see them. Monitor lizards, which grow to a length of about 1.5 m (5 ft), are common along the coast and even inhabit some areas of Mombasa; however, they are harmless. There are many smaller lizards including the colourful agamas (metallic blues and reds), which you are bound to see. Chameleons, too, are fairly common but harmless.

As far as hotels are concerned there is very little of quality in the town itself, apart from the Oceanic Hotel on Mbuyuni Road and the already mentioned Outrigger Hotel. When it comes to restaurants the town is slightly worse off but an excellent meal can be had at the Tamarind, on the Nyali side of the creek facing the old harbour, although it can also be a little pricy. Other suggestions for the town itself are the Oceanic Hotel, which has a casino and, for Chinese food, the Hongkong on Moi Avenue.

As far as nightlife is concerned there is little for the non-sailor apart from the casino and the nearby hotels, particularly on the north coast.

The South Coast

Almost all hotel and resort development south of Mombasa is centred on the stunning Diani Beach, which is about 40 km (25 miles) from

The pace of life is somewhat slower on the coast, and there is plenty of time for relaxation.

Mombasa. The exceptions are Likoni, just across the creek from the town, and Shimoni, which is almost on the Tanzanian border. The whole of the south coast is served by a good road and there is a landing strip for light aircraft at Ukunda on Diani Beach.

Diani Beach itself is 10 km (6 miles) long – a vast uninterrupted stretch of tropical white sand lapped by an opal ocean. The hotels nestle in cleared beachfront areas of the Jadini forest – still the haunt of leopards and colobus monkeys as well as a myriad of forest birds. There are also some private houses available for renting, and several self catering villages.

Most marine activities are available including water skiing, scuba diving, snorkelling and deep sea fishing. The main centre for fishing is Shimoni, 100 km (62 miles) from Mombasa, based on the Pemba Channel Fishing Club. Fishing takes place all the year round except for May, June and perhaps July. Shimoni is also the base for visits to the Kisite-Mpunguti Marine National Park.

Accommodation can be found at the Shelley Beach Hotel, Likoni and, at Diani Beach, at the Golden Beach Hotel, Diani Reef Hotel, Leisure Lodge and Camp, Leopard Beach Hotel, Trade Winds Hotel, Two Fishes Hotel and Jadini Beach Hotel. The Pemba Channel Fishing Club is at Shimoni.

The North Coast

Long stretches of idyllic beaches, fringed with palms, casuarina trees, oleanders and frangipani, make the north coast between Mombasa and Kilifi (72 km, 45 miles from Mombasa) a tourist paradise.

Nyali, the north mainland immediately after crossing the New Nyali Bridge, is a well established garden suburb for Kenya's oldest town. Elegant, air conditioned houses with landscaped gardens are owned by the town's élite. Off the road from the new bridge to Nyali lies the Bahari Beach Club, a major centre for snorkelling, scuba diving, water skiing and big game fishing. Not far beyond, the Moorish lines of the Tamarind restaurant overlook the old harbour. Beyond this the visitor reaches a promontory known as English Point, now marked by cement silos – such is the respect of history – where in the nineteenth century the first colony of liberated slaves was established by the British. It also commemorates the missionary Ludwig von Krapf and his wife, who reached Mombasa in May 1844. Nearby is Moi Park, where the Mombasa Agricultural Society of Kenya Show is held each August.

The Bamburi Beach hotel has one of the best swimming pools of any along the coast.

The privately owned Nyali estate boasts an interesting and beauti-
fully kept golf course, squash and tennis courts, and on its shoreline,
overlooking the pure golden sand, stand some of Kenya's finest beach
hotels.

A nearby attraction is the private wildlife and forest sanctuary,
Bamburi Quarry Farm, established by the Bamburi Cement company to repair the ugly scars left in the landscape after excavating
limestone for cement. It is open daily and admission is free. The vivid

green shrubs and forest are alive with wildlife, and peacocks strut in forested glades beneath eucalyptus, conocarpus, palms and casuarinas on a 26 hectare (65 acre) site. Tilapia and other species of edible fish are bred commercially in ponds to help make the project self supporting.

Shore-bound viewers are able to see the wonders of a snorkelling trip at the Kipepeo Aquarium nearby, with its 150 species of tropical inshore fish on display.

Not far up the coast Mtwapa Creek, with its magnificent cliffs and shimmering placid surface, cuts deep inland. Years ago it was crossed by a hand-hauled chain ferry, with a crew which sang local sea shanties as they pulled the visitors across and which, it is said, inspired at least one Paul Robeson ballad. In 1958 a toll suspension bridge was built some way downstream, and the spot where the ferry had operated has now been turned into a luxury recreational centre and hotel, named Shimo la Tewa – Cave of the rock cod, in Swahili. The suspension bridge has now also gone and has been replaced by a single span road bridge.

Mtwapa is a base for water sports and big game fishing trips out through the opening, over the reef and into the Indian Ocean. It is also the departure point for trips in a dhow which has been converted into a luxurious cruise boat.

On the north side of Mtwapa Creek is the Kenya Marineland, with its tanks filled with sharks, turtles, sting rays and other fish, complete with an intrepid diver who daily plunges in to hand feed the sharks. There is also a serpentarium with a large collection of mambas, cobras, crocodiles and other reptiles. Not far away, on the coastal headland, is one of Kenya's national monuments, dating back five centuries, a slave trading base uncovered in 1972.

A few miles further up is Kikambala, the last of the beach resorts within easy reach of Mombasa.

The next 40 km (25 miles) to Kilifi are covered with vast stretches of sisal, a large fibre crop which is subject to fluctuations in world demand and pricing. Beyond that the road climbs up to the south headlands of Kilifi Creek, which cuts 24 km (15 miles) inland, and provides one of the coast's breathtaking views. The birdlife at the top end of the creek is prolific, providing a colourful display, including concentrations of the magnificent carmine bee-eater. Hotels and marinas provide all water sports plus a 15-minute flight round the creek by seaplane. Kilifi Township, on the north side, is a friendly, neat little community largely populated by Muslims.

Accommodation can be found at the following hotels:

Nyali
Mombasa Beach Hotel, Nyali Beach Hotel, Reef Hotel.

Bamburi
Bamburi Beach Hotel, Neptune Hotel, Severin Sea Lodge, White-sands Hotel.

Shanzu
Intercontinental, Palm Beach Hotel, Serana Beach Hotel.

Kikambala
Sun 'n' Sand Hotel, Whispering Palms Hotel.

Kilifi
Mnarani (Kilifi) Hotel.

Watamu and Gede

Kenya's most notable lost city, a collection of remarkable marine parks and beach resorts, and the ancient and modern quarters of one of its oldest towns have made the area around Malindi, on the north coast and 120 km (75 miles) from Mombasa, one of the fastest-developing holiday centres in Africa.

North of Kilifi the Kenya coast runs virtually straight until the turn-off to Watamu, now a national marine reserve. In the hinterland lies the remains of the Arabuko-Sokoke Forest, now a nature reserve, which contains Kenya's only indigenous rubber trees and is noted for its bird and butterfly life. On the seaward side lies the Watamu reserve, but before reaching it the road passes Gede Village and Kenya's most outstanding national monument, the ruins of Gede, a lost city whose population inexplicably vanished three hundred or more years ago, leaving no clues to their fate, a sort of land-locked African *Marie Celeste*. In its time Gede was a lively centre of Islamic civilization covering almost 20 hectares (50 acres) and with a population of more than two-and-a-half thousand people.

Even today its well-preserved and signposted ruins, with main-tained tracks, do nothing to diminish its air of mystery and brooding stillness. Even as the harsh noon sun strikes down through the surrounding jungle the rustle of monkeys, or the flutter of birds can

Most sunbathing is done in the grounds of the hotels, where shade is available from the fierce heat. This is at the Serena Beach Hotel, one of the best hotels on the northern coast.

make the heart jump. Few people linger in its ruined streets as the sun's shadows lengthen.

They make instead for the delights of Watamu Marine National Park, in addition to which there is a bay filled with islands, and shoreside hotels where the accent is on relaxation.

There is accommodation at the Watamu Beach Hotel, Seafarers, Ocean Sports and the Turtle Bay Hotel.

Malindi

Back-tracking to the main road, and some 16 km (10 miles) further up the coast, is Malindi, the Melind of the seventeenth-century poet,

John Milton, and for centuries a staunch Portuguese ally and outpost for the ships plying the Indies routes round the Cape.

The town's history reputedly goes back 1000 years, but it can only be reliably dated from the thirteenth century by Arabic records and pottery finds.

Many hotels serve the town, with its 8 km (5 mile) curving beach which is a favourite spot for surfing, best in July and August when the monsoons whip the rollers in through the long break in the reef. Casinos and night clubs, Islamic mosques, a colourful market, a nine-hole golf course and, of course, the Malindi Marine National Park, all add to the resort's many attractions. So does the fish market and the sailing club from which stalwarts from all over the world set forth in search of the giants of the sea. Kenya holds several world records for the big game fish of the deeps. Hemingway was one of the many to enjoy the sport here.

All fishing within Malindi Marine National Park, however, is forbidden. So is the removal of shells and corals as it is the coral gardens in the middle of the park, seen either by skin-diving, snorkelling or peering through the hull of a glass-bottomed boat, which fascinate all visitors. Fish of all colours, shapes and sizes, including the octopus and poisonous, ugly stone fish, provide the spectacle.

On the north side of Malindi is an extensive salt pan system for producing sea salt, on an eroded wasteland of sandstone cliffs and precipices known as Hell's Kitchen. Further on is the Arabian Nights' town of Mambrui and its Islamic and Chinese relics; beyond that Ngomeni, a small village and harbour at the entrance to Formosa Bay, which sweeps in a wide curve almost 80 km (50 miles) to the Tana River delta. Great rollers pound in here but, at present, it is not a developed tourist area.

You can find accommodation in the area at the Blue Marlin, Driftwood Club, Palm Tree Club, Sinbad and the Suli Suli Sporting Club.

Lamu and the Lamu Archipelago

Lamu is a town, an island and an archipelago. The town is now well known, a delightful anachronism carrying on its daily life as it has done for centuries, and here the visitors has a strange feeling of being transported back through time.

The islands of the Lamu archipelago – sometimes called the Bajun

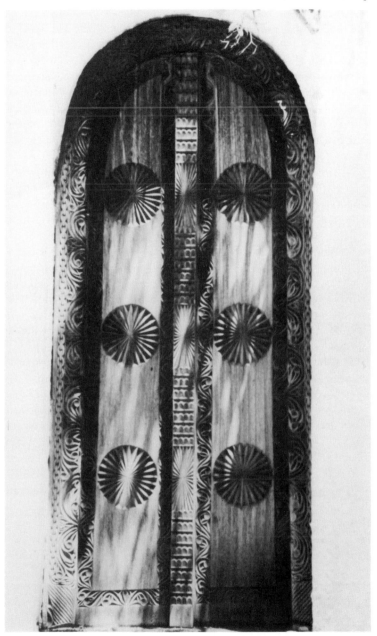

Lamu doors like this one command high prices anywhere in the world.

islands after their sunny inhabitants – lie close to the Kenya mainland in a broken chain reaching almost to the Somali border. Some of
the islands hide years and years of history, for there are numerous
archaeological sites, some as yet uncovered, which date as far back as
the ninth century. Other islands, Kiwayuu for instance, have not
only the allure of isolation but, when found, reveal a stunning
tropical beauty. Others seem scarcely to have reached the twentieth
century, for time means nothing. Visiting the ancient town of Lamu,
with its cloistered streets, forbidding walls of age-worn coral, is like
stepping into life exactly as it was two centuries ago.

Settlements here date back to the fourteenth century, and by the
nineteenth century Lamu was a flourishing, licentious community;
but labour emigration to the bigger cities and a fall in exports in the
early part of this century brought an end to its heyday. There is still
evidence of the elegant, refined life led by the richer members of the
population in the past. If you can be shown the interiors of some of
the grander mansions – rather drab on the outside as the rich didn't
want to advertise their wealth to the frequent raiders – you will find
enormously intricate plasterwork unknown in the rest of Islam. The
architecture is also interesting as it is admirably suited to the
climate – a series of open-plan galleries almost always without doors,
and interior courtyards open to the sky, which ensures shade and
calm against the tropical sun.

Both the Swahili and the Bajuni who people the town and the
archipelago have a great tradition of craftsmanship. Gold and silver
ornaments, tooled leather work, hand-illuminated Korans and boat
building are all examples. But pride of place must go to wood
carving, especially the great carved doorways which provide relief
from the awesome uniformity of the exterior of the houses.

A visit to Lamu involves not simply the excitement of discovery,
but a lesson in living. Apart from one vehicle, which rarely moves and
then only for half a mile, the internal combustion engine is
absent – no cars are allowed, although the donkey population is large.
It's a tranquil life and people frequently smile and have seemingly
endless time to talk. The simplicity and grace of existence is totally
therapeutic.

Travel to Lamu is easiest by light aircraft, but a good road
connects Malindi with Lamu and there is a secure car park where the
road ends at Mkowe. Accommodation in Lamu is generally simple
but adequate and is always compensated for by the ambience and
locale.

The town, however, is not by any means all that the area has to offer. The district is a microcosm of all that is good in Kenya's tourism: beautiful sea, tropical beaches, antiques, game, marine pursuits and friendly people. Enterprising tour operators have now made it possible to visit not only the town but to sail the archipelago, reaching the Kiunga Marine Park and the Dodori National Reserve on the land.

For desert island lovers there are two remote hideaways on Kiwayuu and Manda which are the ultimate in getting away from it all. Those who must pursue the trail to the end will find at Ishakani, just short of the Somali border, some fifteenth and sixteenth century ruins comparable with any in the world.

The choice of accommodation is as follows:

On Lamu Island
New Mahrus Hotel, Peponi Hotel and Petley's Inn.

On Manda Island
Ras Kitau Beach Hotel.

On Kiwayuu
Kiwayuu Island Lodge.

Near Mkokoni
Kiwayuu Safari Lodge.

9 The Great Rift Valley and the Mountains of Kenya

The Great Rift Valley has been described as a scar on the face of the Earth, a not unreasonable description as it is one of the few natural features that can be picked out from space. It is certainly one of the wonders of the world and one's first sight is always unforgettable. Mine, like many before, was the view from the Nairobi to Naivasha road as I climbed the edge of the Aberdare Range of hills. Below me to the left was the Kedong Valley, the floor of the Rift, and rising out of it in smouldering magnificence were the two semi-active volcanic peaks of Mt Nyukie and Mt Longonot. Across the heat shimmer could be seen the other side of the valley, and the Mau Escarpment which seems to rise vertically from the floor, giving a valuable clue as to how it was formed.

The Rift is a 6500 km (4000 mile) fault line running from Jordan in the north, through the Red Sea and Ethiopia. From here on it is a 50 km (30-mile) wide trench, dipping below sea level in places, as it continues through Kenya, Tanzania, Mozambique on to Lake Nyasa in Malawi.

Although there has been some activity in the region for many millions of years and the major elements of the Great Rift Valley were formed within the last 20 million years, there has been considerable activity in the region during the last 10,000 years which probably led to the forming of the Red Sea. To back this up there are claims that the ancestors of the Somalis travelled from Africa to Arabia over dry land across the straits of Bab-el-Mandeb, at the southern tip of the Red Sea. Legends such as this were first heard in the 1880s when exploration of the area began.

A German naturalist, Dr Gustav Fischer, was the first white person to enter Masailand, in 1883, where the most spectacular features of the Rift are. He reached Lake Naivasha, but later in the same year Joseph Thomson, the British explorer, went as far north as Lake

The tranquil waters of Lake Baringo attract ornithologists as well as those who just want to get away from it all.

Baringo, revealing the extent of the Rift. Four years later the Hungarian, Count Teleki, went even further north, arriving at a huge watery expanse which he named Lake Rudolph after the Austrian crown prince. (It is now Lake Turkana.) The discovery of Lake Rudolph was very important to the geologists of the day who could now point to a line of lakes, running towards the Red Sea and pointing to the fact that the Rift was one united geological feature.

Another important man of the day was John Walter Gregory, who confirmed the Rift as one feature by painstaking fieldwork, and it was he who coined the name The Great Rift Valley. Since his day geologists have gradually been building up data and now a picture of its formation has been agreed.

The first recognizable activity that formed the rift was roughly 40 million years ago, when great lakes appeared, probably forerunners of today's smaller ones. A mere 11 million years ago there was the main faulting, followed in the last three million years by other faulting on the valley floor. Just one million years ago the valley's shoulders were pushed up, a by-product of which are the fabulous views enjoyed today by visitors to the area. All these movements produced intense volcanic activity as the subsidence of the floor, due to continental drift, caused the molten rock beneath to be squeezed up at the sides. This volcanic activity still continues, and the Red Sea and the Gulf of Aden are gradually widening, with the possibility that one day East Africa will be torn apart and the Great Rift Valley will sometime in the future become an ocean.

Unlike the plateaux on either side of the Rift, which consist of rock around 3000 million years old, the valley surface itself is quite young, being covered with volcanic ash rich in sodium carbonate (washing soda), much of which has found its way into the lakes making them bitter, and some of them into soda lakes. Few animals have adapted to these conditions, the major exception being the flamingo.

Lakes Magadi and Natron

The two lakes that lie in the hottest and deepest trough in the Kenyan section of the Rift are Magadi in Kenya and Natron in Tanzania, and consequently are major producers of soda. Both lack an outlet and much of the water that reaches them is already very alkaline. Even rain water that runs off the surrounding hills is alkaline from volcanic ash emitted by Ol Doinyo Lengai, an active volcano that has a white alkaline crust ringing its crater. Its nearby springs are also rich in the mineral, all of which combines to give the lakes little chance of clear water.

Magadi is very arid, with only 40 cm (16 in) of rain falling on it in an average year. However, in a year around 330 cm (130 in) of water evaporates, concentrating the alkali solution. The flamingos are the only wildlife able to feed off these lakes. Much further north is Lake Turkana, the largest of the lakes in Kenya, but it too is bitter in parts, although much less so than the extremes of Magadi and Natron. Its shores partly consist of volcanoes and therefore soda does run into it; however, fresh water from the River Omo feeds into the lake, diluting the soda and preventing it concentrating with evaporation. The waters of the lake are just on the threshold of life-giving and allow larger forms of life besides fish to develop.

The Flamingo

Whatever else inhabits the length and breadth of the Great Rift Valley, the big success story is the flamingo. Of the five million in the world around two-thirds live in the Rift Valley, most of them in Kenya. In this part of the world there are just two of the six species – the greater and lesser flamingos. Apart from differences in the plumage and beak they are, as one would expect, the largest and smallest of the flamingos, with the greater (comprising only about 50,000 in number) standing nearly 2 m (6 ft) tall, with the lesser around 1 m (3 ft) tall.

They range wherever there are soda lakes, but their true home is Lake Nakuru (see also Chapter 6, The Game Parks) where it is possible to see up to two million flamingos. It has been called the greatest bird spectacle in the world – and rightly deserves the accolade. Most of the shoreline has been incorporated into a national park by the Kenyan Government. The park is a strip, varying between a few hundred metres and 3 km (2 miles) wide, that runs beside the lake for most of its circumference. Next to it is the Baharini Sanctuary, a beautiful area of shoreline and acacia woodland that was once the farm of John Hopcraft, who has dedicated his land and his life to the study and protection of Lake Nakuru and its birds.

The explanation of what draws the flamingos to Lake Nakuru is simple – food. The algae *spirulina*, which is there in incredible concentrations, is the mainstay of the flamingo, and it supports the large populations of brine shrimps and other small crustacea, also a useful food supply. The soda-saturated water produces the food faster than the birds are able to consume it, which they do at a rate of about 200 tons a day. Another important factor is sunlight, a commodity in which Lake Nakuru is also rich. It stands 1700 m (5700 feet) above sea level and very close to the equator, so is bathed in ultra violet rays year round. However, the water is lethal for the birds so they have developed a pumping and straining process. When they need to drink they go to a fresh water lake of which there are some nearby.

The flamingo has a rather awkward looking beak bending sharply half-way down its length. It uses this section as a ladle, feeding with its head upside down. Opening the beak slightly it sucks in water, before pumping it out with its tongue. A series of bristles on the inside of the beak exclude large objects entering the beak and as the water is being pumped out smaller, finer bristles trap the food particles. The food contains a substance called canthaxanthin, which is similar to Vitamin A and which turns the flamingo pink. Once away from these lakes it reverts to white unless fed synthetic canthaxanthin.

Futher north Lake Turkana, or the Jade Sea as it is also known, is one of the most uncompromising and severe landscapes of the Rift Valley. The sandy western shores are almost barren except where fresh water springs well up to produce an oasis of palms. The other side is quite different being rocky and broken up by green reed beds where the larger wild animals of the area, such as lion, zebra and waterbuck come to drink. Behind it, though, the terrain is merciless, with just dry scrub to break up the monotony of the landscape. At the southern end of this long lake there is nothing but lifeless volcanic rocks and razar sharp lava.

However, the wealth of fossils that litter the landscape demonstrates the plentiful wildlife that once walked these shores. There are also ample fossils which show that the earliest tool-using man lived in this unlikely corner of the world. As in Pompeii, it is the volcanic ash that has preserved the fossils, and the remains that we are now examining open a window into man's past. At the same time the constant shifting of the Rift, producing lakes and then obliterating them, captured and preserved bones until further upheavals exposed them again.

The Great Rift Valley in the area here is known as the Cradle of Mankind following Richard Leakey's discovery of the skull of *Australopithecus*. The shattered cranium with human characteristics was discovered simply lying on the ground, having been washed out by recent rains. The original owner of the skull was probably about 1.5 m (5 ft) tall with a low forehead, large eyebrows and a small brain about the size of a gorilla's. Its molars were twice the width of our own, suggesting grinding teeth used by the vegetarian. This particular avenue of human evolution did probably not evolve further, but the quantity of stone tools and an axe head dated at 2.5 million years, found in the area, means that there was early intelligent life at Lake Turkana.

The scattered tribes that now live along the shores use survival

Nyahururu (formerly Thomsons) Falls is one of the dramatic evidences of faulting along the Great Rift Valley.

techniques that in some cases are not all that different from those of the early hunters. True, there is now iron where there was once stone, but most tribes are nomadic with individual property being restricted to a herd of camels, cattle, goats or sheep. Although there is some fishing, only one tribe makes ends meet with food from the lake, the El Molo; a literal translation of their name is the People Who Live by Catching Fish. It is an irony that this cradle of mankind can now barely support a few dwindling tribes.

The Mountains

Further south are the mountains of Kenya which, without doubt, offer some of the finest hill and mountain expeditions to be found anywhere in the world. Although many of the ascents are an easy day's climb some are very arduous due to the terrain, their length, altitude and the heat. The former can be climbed by the holiday-maker, but the latter should be left to the professional.

Travel on the highest mountains such as Mount Kenya, the Aberdares and Mount Elgon should not be attempted during the rainy seasons when conditions may become very difficult; however, don't lose heart if you wish to make a small climb because the rains are not uninterrupted. Although Kenyan weather is notoriously good, there are distinct seasonal changes. Over the western Kenyan highlands rain occurs from March or April to September or October. Most of the highlands area east of the Aberdare range has two rainy seasons. Here the long rains falls from March or April until mid-May. The secondary short rains are from late October to mid-December. In this eastern region there are also two dry seasons, from June to September when it is cool and cloudy, and from January to March when it is sunny and warm. Generally the rain is in the form of showers or heavy thunderstorms broken by several hours of sunshine. In the highlands the mornings are usually fine, with the rain occurring during the afternoons and evenings.

Early exploration

Kilimanjaro

Mount Kilimanjaro, nestling in Tanzania on the Kenyan border, was the first of the two great mountains of the region to be seen, explored and climbed by Europeans. It was a missionary, Rebmann, who first sighted the mountain on 11 May 1848, although reports of a mountain with a white cap had been mentioned to the early explorers. He recorded his discovery in the *Church Missionary Intelligencer* in May 1849, but was ridiculed by the pundits of the day, who refused to believe that snow existed so close to the equator. However, it wasn't long after that British travellers pushing westward soon confirmed that Kilimanjaro and its snowy mantle did indeed exist. But it wasn't till 1862 that the first European steps were to be seen on the higher slopes.

Mount Kenya

In 1849 Rebmann's colleague, Johann Krapf, claimed to have seen another snow capped mountain, but this was too much for the establishment, who derided Krapf. Imagine their surprise in 1883 when Joseph Thomson also reported seeing the mountain, passing close enough to make a positive identification of snow. Four years later Count Teleki climbed to 4270 m (14,000 ft) and in 1893 J. Gregory ascended the glacier zone to about 4700 m (15,500 ft). Finally, in 1899, Batian, the highest peak on Mount Kenya, was climbed; the second highest peak, Nelion, was not climbed until 1929, 80 years after the mountain was first seen by Europeans.

The presence of snow capped mountains in Africa was suspected more than 2000 years ago. In the second century Ptolemy, that great traveller, inscribed on his map the *Montes Lunae* (Mountains of the Moon) from whose waters flowed the great lakes that fed the Nile. Soon after Kilimanjaro and Kenya were seen it was suggested that these must be the Mountains of the Moon; however, this was later proved not to be so as they were separated from the Nile by the Great Rift Valley.

Many of the mountains of Kenya lie in the vast extent of the country over which the Masai have ruled for more than a hundred years. For a long time the reputation of the tribe kept Europeans out of their lands, although information did leak out, particularly during the mid-eighteenth century when Arab and Swahili traders sent caravans into the interior, mostly for slave trading.

Of the larger East African mountains below the snow line, one of the most interesting is Mount Elgon, which lies on the borders of Kenya and Uganda. The first European to see Mount Elgon may have been the British explorer Sir Henry Morton Stanley–the man who found Livingstone. He named it Masaba, although he didn't find the huge Masai Caves now occupied by elephants and their lookouts, the bats. Mount Elgon isn't called the loneliest park in Kenya for nothing, so it's best not to take too many risks when looking round the caves.

Many of the lesser mountains of East Africa are also of interest and the Taita Hills in Tsavo, south-east of Nairobi, are particularly good examples of ranges which have supported pastoral populations for as long as we have records and back into tribal memory. Further north, south east of Lake Turkana, the mountains of Marsabit provide relief from the arid surroundings and ample food and water supplies. When Lord Delamere arrived in this area in 1896 on a reconnaissance mission, and when the Samburu were in possession of the mountain, it still swarmed with elephant. One of his companions shot 21 elephants in 21 days – an example not to be followed by modern visitors to the area.

10 Useful Swahili Words and Phrases

Here are just a few useful words. It is not possible to give a comprehensive guide here, but it is worth remembering that Swahili is a phonetic language and most consonants are pronounced hard. It uses the standard alphabet. As with everyone else, the Kenyans appreciate it if you try to speak their language, although almost everybody speaks English in some way or another.

General

Hallo	Jambo
How are you?	Habari?
Well	Mzuri
Bad	Mbaya
Thank you (very much)	Asante (sana)
Please	Tafadhali
Goodbye	Kwaheri
Welcome	Karibu
Danger	Hatari
Friend	Rafiki
Sorry	Pole
Yes	Naam
No	La
I want	Nataka
How much?	Pesa ngapi?
Big	Kubwa
Small	Kidogo
Quickly	Upesi
Slowly	Polepole
Doctor	Dokitari
Hospital	Hospitali

Bar and Restaurant

Beer	Tembo
Bread	Mkate
Butter	Siagi
Chicken	Kuku
Coffee	Kahawa
Egg(s)	Yai (Mayai)
Fish	Samaki
Food	Chakula
Meat	Nyama
Milk	Maziwa
Onion	Kitunguru
Potatoes	Viazi
Salt	Chumvi
Sugar	Sukari
Sweet	Tamu
Tea	Chai
Vegetables	Mboga
Warm	Moto
Water	Maji

Numbers

One	Moja	Thirty	Thelathini
Two	Mbili	Forty	Arobaini
Three	Tatu	Fifty	Hamsini
Four	Nne	Sixty	Sitini
Five	Tano	Seventy	Sabini
Six	Sita	Eighty	Themanini
Seven	Saba	Ninety	Tisini
Eight	Nane	One hundred	Mia
Nine	Tisa	Two hundred	Mia mbili
Ten	Kumi	Nine hundred and	Mia tisa tisini
Eleven	Kumi na moja	ninety-nine	na tisa
Twenty	Ishirini	One thousand	Elfu
Twenty one	Ishirini na moja		

Time

Monday	Jumatutu	Daytime	Mchana
Tuesday	Jumanne	Morning	Asubuhi
Wednesday	Jumatono	Afternoon	Alasiri
Thursday	Alhamisi	Evening	Jioni
Friday	Ijumaa	Day	Siku
Saturday	Jumamosi	Week	Wiki
Sunday	Jumapili	Month	Mwezi
Today	Leo	Year	Mwaka
Tomorrow	Kesho		
Yesterday	Jana		
Night	Usiku		

(The names of the months sound
almost the same as in English

Everyday Words

Money	Fedha	Shoes	Viatu
Expensive	Ghali	Bring	Lete
Cheap	Rahisi	May I have	Tafadhali nipe
Shop	Duka	I want	Ninataka
Market	Soko	What is your name?	Jina lako nani?
Post Office	Posa	Call a policeman	Mwite polisi
Bank	Benki	I am lost	Nimepotea
Hotel	Hoteli	Taxi	Taksi
Cigarettes	Sigareti	Stop here	Simama hapa
Newspaper	Gazeti	Wait here	Ngoja hapa
Clothes	Nguo	Where is the toilet?	Choo iko wapi?

Game Animals

Baboon/monkey	Nyani
Buffalo	Nyati
Cheetah	Duma
Elephant	Tembo
Giraffe	Twiga
Hippo	Kiboko
Hyena	Fisi
Impala	Swara
Leopard	Chui
Lion	Simba
Rhino	Kifaru
Warthog	Ngiri
Zebra	Punda milia

Bibliography

ADAMSON, JOY, *Born Free*, Fontana, 1970.

BERLITZ, *Swahili for Travellers*, Cassell, 1974.

BLIXEN, KAREN, *Out of Africa*, Penguin, 1954.

BOCK, DR K., *A Guide to Common Reef Fishes of the Western Indian Ocean*, Macmillan.

CHURCHILL, WINSTON: *My African Journey*, Hodder & Stoughton, 1908.

ELDON, KATHY, *Eating Out*.

FEDDERS/SALVADOR, *Peoples and Cultures of Kenya*, Collings, 1981.

GREGORY, J.W., *The Great Rift Valley*, Cass, 1968.

HUXLEY, ELSPETH, *The Flame Trees of Thika*, Chatto, 1959.

—, —, *Mottled Lizard*, Chatto, 1962.

KENYATTA, JOMO, *Facing Mount Kenya*, Heinemann, 1979.

LUGARD, F. D., *The Rise of Our East African Empire*, Cass, 1968.

MABERLY, C. T. ASTLEY, *Animals of East Africa*, Hodder & Stoughton.

MILLER, CHARLES, *The Lunatic Express*, Futura, 1977.

MITCHELL, VIVIEN, *History of the Safari Rally*, Nairobi Space Publications.

MOLLISON, SIMON, *Kenya's Coast*, East African Publishing House, 1971.

OJIAMBO, J. A., *The Trees of Kenya*, Kenya Literature Bureau, 1978.

PATTERSON, J. H., *Man-Eaters of Tsavo*, Macmillan, 1979.

RIEFENSTAHL, LENI, *Coral Gardens*, Collins, 1978.

ROBSON, PETER, *Mountains of Kenya*, West Col, 1976.

RODWELL, EDWARD, *Coast Causerie*, Rodwell Press.

ROOSEVELT, THEODORE, *African Game Trails*, Scribner, 1910.

THOMSON, JOSEPH, *Through Masai Land*, Cass, 1968.

TOMKINSON, MICHAEL, *Kenya: a holiday guide*, M. Tomkinson.

Index